W9-AYR-952

A CLASSIC RETELLING

The ODYSSEY

by Homer

nextext

WOSU-Sayre / McMahan Library

Cover photograph: Tony Stone Images

Copyright © 2000 by Nextext®, an imprint of McDougal Littell, a Houghton Mifflin Company. All rights reserved.

No part of this work may be reproduced or transmitted in any form or by any means, electronic or mechanical, including photocopying and recording, or by any information storage or retrieval system without prior written permission of Nextext® unless such copying is expressly permitted by federal copyright law. With the exception of not-for-profit transcription in Braille, Nextext® is not authorized to grant permission for further uses of copyrighted selections reprinted in this text without the permission of their owners. Permission must be obtained from the individual copyright owners identified herein. Address inquiries to Manager, Rights and Permissions, McDougal Littell, P. O. Box 1667, Evanston, Illinois 60204.

Printed in China

ISBN-13: 978-0-618-00372-3

ISBN-10: 0-618-00372-X

9 10 11   0940   11 10 09

883
H7520

Table of Contents

*Vocabulary words appear in boldface type and are
footnoted. Specialized or technical words and phrases
appear in lightface type and are footnoted.*

Background

The Story of *The Iliad* and *The Odyssey*

The Iliad is the story about the last four days of the Trojan War. The war began after a young man named Paris stole Helen of Troy from her husband, Menelaus. The Greeks promised to help Menelaus fight for Helen, and they sent a thousand ships with him to Troy, including a ship with Odysseus on board.

But the city of Troy was well defended, and the battle went on for ten years. Odysseus helped decide the war when he tricked the Trojans. He and his men built a huge wooden horse. Greek soldiers were hidden inside the horse, which was left outside the gate of the city of Troy as a gift. Once the horse was pulled inside the walls of Troy, the Greeks were at last able to enter the city and help win the battle.

The Odyssey tells the story of Odysseus, who had left Troy after the war with twelve ships and more than 700 men. Yet only Odysseus returned home to Ithaca after many adventures and much sorrow.

Epics

Both The Iliad and The Odyssey are epic poems that tell stories about Greek heroes and gods. An epic is a long adventure story about a hero. Epic stories tell about values and ideals of a country or people. Like The Iliad, The Odyssey was probably sung as a series of popular songs.

People read epic stories to learn about great heroes of long ago and their ideals. Odysseus, for example, is famous for tricking his enemies. He is cunning and sly, but also a noble and brave hero.

Main Characters in *The Odyssey*

Gods and Goddesses

Zeus,
king of the gods and ruler of
the sky

Poseidon,
king of the sea and brother of Zeus

Hades,
ruler of the house of the dead

Athena,
daughter of Zeus, goddess
of intelligence, the arts, and war

Hermes,
messenger of the gods

Lesser Gods

Calypso,
an island nymph on Ogygian who
holds Odysseus prisoner

Circe,
daughter of the sun, goddess of
the wild

Aeolus,
keeper of the winds

◀ **Hades**

Sirens ▶

Family of Odysseus

Laertes,
father of Odysseus

Penelope,
wife of Odysseus

Telemachus,
son of Odysseus and Penelope

Eumaeus,
keeper of Odysseus's pigs who
gives him a place to stay when
he returns to Ithaca

Euryclea,
an old nurse of Odysseus's who
knows him by the scar on his leg

Monsters

Polyphemus,
a giant Cyclops who is blinded
by Odysseus

Sirens,
beauties who seduce men with
their singing

Scylla,
a six-headed monster and
man-eater

Charybdis,
a whirlpool that sinks ships

Story Within a Story

The "story" of *The Odyssey* is a simple one:

Telemachus goes in search of his father, who left twenty years before to fight in the Trojan War, but doesn't find him. ┈┈▶ Odysseus is a prisoner of Calypso, but is freed by the gods. ┈┈▶ Odysseus's return takes him first to the land of the Phaeacians, ruled by King Alcinous, to whom he tells his story. ┈┈

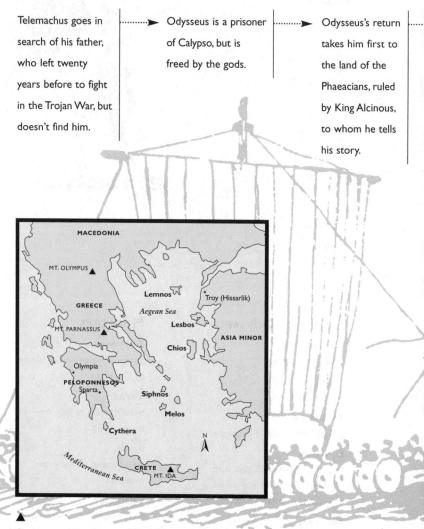

Greece and the Aegean World in ancient times.

In the middle of the book, Odysseus tells King Alcinous the story of his earlier adventures, creating a story within a story. He tells of adventures that took place in an earlier time on his return voyage after the war in Troy. Here is a list of his adventures.

Adventures of Odysseus

1. Fought in Trojan War
2. Sacked island of Ismarus
3. Blown to land of the Lotus-eaters
4. Visited land of the Cyclops
5. Blown off course by Aeolus's bag of winds
6. Journeyed to land of giant Laestrygonians
7. Visited Circe, who turned men into pigs
8. Journeyed to Hades to speak to the ghosts of the dead
9. Sailed by the Sirens
10. Slipped by Scylla and Charybdis

Odysseus returns to Ithaca in disguise and kills the suitors who are trying to marry his wife.

Homer

Almost nothing is known about Homer, who is said to be the author of *The Odyssey*. Scholars have suggested many ideas about who he was and what he wrote, but little is known for certain. He may have "created" the stories of *The Iliad* and *The Odyssey*, even if he did not actually write them down. Long ago, stories were passed from one generation to the next. Scholars believe Homer pulled together a number of stories that had been handed down over the years.

Homer may also have been blind and may have worked as a storyteller, singing tales of Odysseus and other Greek heroes. His stories were sung at festivals all over Greece and learned by children. And, ever since that time, *The Odyssey* has been told again and again.

A CLASSIC RETELLING

The ODYSSEY

BOOK I

This is the story of Odysseus, the most famous of heroes and the mastermind of war. Odysseus left his home in Ithaca many years ago to fight in the Trojan War. He has been wandering ever since. The gods agree that it is time for him to go home. His wife and son do not know if he will ever return. Men who want to marry Penelope, Odysseus's wife, are living in his house.

What happened to that hero, Odysseus? He traveled to faraway cities and fought in many battles. He suffered many hardships. Others who fought with him have all returned home. All but Odysseus have returned.

He longed to return to his wife and country, but Odysseus was held captive by the goddess

Calypso.[1] She had imprisoned him in a large cave and wanted to marry him. Years went by, until the time when the gods decided that he should go back to **Ithaca.**[2] But Poseidon, god of the sea, would not let him go home.

Poseidon was still mad at Odysseus for having blinded his son, king of the **Cyclops.**[3] Instead of killing Odysseus, Poseidon **tortured**[4] him by preventing him from getting home.

So the gods sent Hermes to the island where Odysseus was held by Calypso to tell her that they had made up their minds and that Odysseus was to return home.

So **Athena**,[5] with her glittering golden sandals, darted from the topmost place on **Olympus.**[6] She went directly to Ithaca and disguised herself as an old friend of Odysseus's. There she found the **suitors**[7] seated on skins of the oxen, which they had

---

[1] **Calypso**—a goddess who lived on an island and held Odysseus prisoner.

[2] **Ithaca**—Odysseus's home.

[3] **Cyclops**—giants with one eye.

[4] **tortured**—to create or give someone much pain.

[5] **Athena**—daughter of Zeus, one of the twelve great gods. She is goddess of war.

[6] **Olympus**—the place where the gods lived.

[7] **suitors**—men who wanted to marry Penelope, thinking her husband was dead.

killed and eaten. They were drinking and eating freely in Odysseus's house.

Telemachus[8] saw Athena before anyone else did. He was thinking about his brave father and about how to send these men out of his house. He caught sight of the stranger (in truth it was Athena dressed like a captain among soldiers) and went straight to her. He said, "Welcome to our house. After you have eaten, you shall tell us for what you have come."

After they had had enough to eat and drink, the music and dancing began. Then Telemachus spoke in a low voice to Athena, with his head close to hers so that no one might hear.

"If these men," said he, "were to see my father come back to Ithaca, they would run from here in fear. What do you know of my father Odysseus?"

And Athena (in disguise) answered: "I will tell you truly. I am **Mentes**,[9] son of Anchialus and a friend of your father. I have come here with my ship and crew. From strangers I heard your father was at home again. That is why I came here. It seems the gods are still keeping him back, for he

---

[8] **Telemachus**—son of Odysseus and Penelope.

[9] Athena calls herself Mentes here, because she's dressed as a stranger. Gods and goddesses often disguise themselves.

is not dead. It is more likely he is on some faraway island or a prisoner among **savages.**[10] I promise you he will not be away much longer."

"My mother," said Telemachus, "tells me I am son to Odysseus, but I was too young to know him when he left home. I hear there is no more unlucky man under heaven than my father."

And Athena said: "Tell me, and tell me true, what is the meaning of all this feasting, and who are these people? What is it all about? And the guests—how badly they are behaving!"

"It seems the gods are still keeping him back, for he is not dead. It is more likely he is on some faraway island or a prisoner among savages. I promise you he will not be away much longer."

Telemachus said, "The gods have given my father and his house these sufferings. I could bear it if he were dead. If he had died in battle with his men at Troy, then he would be honored as a hero. But now we do not know what has happened to him. And, these men of Ithaca are eating up all of the food in the house. They come here to court my mother and ask her to marry them. She is waiting

---

[10] **savages**—rude or brutal persons.

still for Odysseus and will not marry yet. So, they eat their way through all I have."

"Is that so?" exclaimed Athena. "Then you do indeed want Odysseus home again. If Odysseus is the man he once was, then these men will have a sorry time. He will drive them all from his house or murder them. Tell the suitors to go home, each to his own place. If your mother's mind is set on marrying again, let her go back to her father, who will find her a husband.

> *"If Odysseus is the man he once was, then these men will have a sorry time. He will drive them all from his house or murder them."*

"As for yourself, find the best ship you can get. With a crew of twenty men, go in search of your father. If you hear that your father is alive and on his way home, return and help him drive these men out of your house. If you hear of his death, come home at once. Give him a proper funeral and make your mother marry again. Then, having done all this, think how you will kill these suitors. You are a fine, smart-looking fellow. Make a great name for yourself. Show your bravery. And, remember what I have said to you."

Telemachus answered, "It has been good of you to talk to me. I will do all you tell me. I know you want to get on with your voyage, but stay a little longer."

Athena answered, "Do not try to keep me, for I must be on my way at once."

With these words Athena flew away like a bird. She had given Telemachus courage and made him think more than ever about his father. He felt a change in himself. He knew that the stranger had been a god, so he went straight to where the suitors were sitting to follow the instructions he had been given.

Telemachus spoke. "Know," he cried, "by Zeus himself that you shall pay in full when Odysseus returns."

The suitors bit their lips as they heard him and admired his boldness. Then Antinous, son of Eupeithes, said, "The gods seem to have made you brave. Go away, child. You cannot back up such bold words."

Telemachus answered: "Nevertheless, I will be chief in my own house some day."

Then Eurymachus, son of Polybus, answered: "It rests with heaven to decide who shall be chief among us."

"My father may be dead or he may still return after these many years," answered Telemachus. "I must find out if he still lives." With that he left and went alone to his room, thinking of the advice that Athena had given him.

BOOK II

Telemachus tells the suitors to stop wasting his supplies of food and drink and to leave his house. They laugh at him. That night, Telemachus sets sail for Pylos in search of his father.

When the rosy-fingered dawn appeared, Telemachus rose and dressed himself. He left his room looking like an immortal god.[1] He at once called the people in the house around him. When he took his father's seat, everyone made way for him.

Aegyptius, an old man, was the first to speak. His son Antiphus had gone with Odysseus to Troy, but had been killed when the savage Cyclops cooked him for dinner.

"Men of Ithaca," he said, "hear my words. From the day Odysseus left us, there has been no

---

[1] immortal god—being who cannot die.

meeting of us until now. Who then can it be that wants so much to talk with us?"

Telemachus took this speech as a good **omen**.[2] He rose at once, for he was bursting with what he had to say. He stood in the middle of the group and said, "Sir, it is I who asked you to come here. Two great misfortunes have fallen upon my house. The first is the loss of my excellent father. He was like a father to every one of you here. The second is much more serious. It is the **utter**[3] ruin of my wealth and home. You suitors are all **pestering**[4] my mother to marry you against her will. You are afraid to go to her father Icarius to ask him to choose the one he likes best, but day by day you keep hanging about my father's house. You kill our oxen, sheep, and fat goats. You drink all of our wine. I cannot stand this any longer."

With this, Telemachus dashed his staff to the ground, his eyes grown bright with tears. Everyone was very sorry for him. Only Antinous, son of Eupeithes and leader of the suitors, spoke:

"Telemachus, how dare you try to throw the blame upon us suitors? It is your mother's fault, not ours. For more than three years she has not

---

[2] **omen**—a sign of what is to come; a sign of good or bad luck.

[3] **utter**—complete.

[4] **pestering**—bothering, annoying.

made up her mind which one of us to choose. She has told us that she must weave a shroud for Laertes, your grandfather, before she marries again. 'Let me finish my weaving before I marry.' So every day she works on the great **loom**[5] weaving the shroud—but every night she **unravels**[6] that day's work. One of her maids told us so. But understand that we will not go back to our land until she has made her choice and married one of us."

Telemachus answered: "Antinous, how can I drive the mother who bore me from my father's house? My father is **abroad**.[7] We do not know whether he is alive or dead. If you do not stop, **Zeus**[8] shall punish you."

As Telemachus spoke, Zeus sent two eagles from the top of the mountain. They flew over the group and made them afraid. The eagles surely were a sign from the gods.

One of the old men rose and said, "Hear me, men of Ithaca. Odysseus is not going to be away much longer. Indeed after nineteen years

---

[5] **loom**—a tool for making thread or yarn into cloth.

[6] **unravels**—takes apart.

[7] **abroad**—out of one's own country.

[8] **Zeus**—he is the most powerful god on Olympus.

away, he is close at hand to deal out death and destruction. Put a stop to this wickedness before he comes."

One suitor then said: "I can read these omens myself much better than you. Birds are always flying about in the sunshine. Odysseus has died in a far country, and it is a pity you are not dead along with him."

Then Telemachus said: "I shall say no more. Give me a ship and a crew of twenty men to take me in search of my father. I will go to Sparta and to Pylos in search of him. Someone may tell me something. If I hear he is alive and on his way home, I will put up with you suitors for yet another twelve months. If, on the other hand, I hear of his death, I will return at once and make my mother marry another husband."

After the speeches ended, every man went back to his house, except the suitors who returned to the house of Odysseus. Telemachus went alone to the seaside and prayed.

"Hear me," he cried, "O god of yesterday. I would obey you, but the wicked suitors will not let me do so."

Athena was nearby and came to him. "Telemachus," she said, "if you are made of the same stuff as your father, set sail to find him.

Your voyage will not be wasted. Sons are seldom as good men as their fathers—they are generally worse, not better. Still, be neither a fool nor coward. Give no thought to the suitors; they know nothing of the doom that will shortly fall on all of them."

"Your voyage will not be wasted. Sons are seldom as good men as their fathers—they are generally worse, not better. "

Thus spoke Athena, daughter of Zeus. Telemachus lost no time in doing as the goddess told him. He went home to get food for his voyage. The suitors were again eating and drinking wildly. They laughed at him.

"Telemachus," said one, "thinks he can bring friends from Pylos to help him. Good luck."

This was how the suitors talked. But Telemachus went to one of his servants to get food and drink for his voyage. When the servant heard his plan, she began to cry. She said to him, "My dear child, why sail off now? You are the one hope of the house. Your poor father is probably dead and gone in some faraway country. These wicked ones will only try to take everything they can. They will also probably try to kill you if you return. Do not go off wandering across the ocean."

"Fear not," said Telemachus. "Say nothing about all this to my mother until I have been away ten or twelve days." The old woman said she would not say anything.

Meanwhile, Athena took the shape of Telemachus and went round the town to get a crew. When the sun had set and darkness was over all the land, she made a ship and crew ready.

Then she went to the house of Odysseus and threw the suitors into a deep sleep. "Telemachus," said she, "the men are on board and at their oars. **Make haste**[9] and be off."

With these words she led him to the ship. Thus, the ship sped off at night, leaving Ithaca in search of Odysseus.

---

[9] **make haste**—hurry.

BOOK III

Nestor gives Telemachus a warm welcome in Pylos. Nestor tells stories of his own return and that of the other heroes from Troy, but he knows nothing of the fate of Odysseus. Telemachus then goes on to Sparta.

As the sun was rising from the sea, they reached Pylos. The people of Pylos were at the shore. They were having a **festival**[1] to honor Poseidon, lord of the sea. Telemachus and his crew arrived and brought their ship to anchor. Then, slowly and carefully, they went ashore.

The goddess Athena, looking like Mentor, led the way. She said to Telemachus, "You must not be

---

[1] **festival**—a day or special time to rejoice, usually in memory of someone or something.

shy or **nervous**.[2] You have voyaged from Ithaca to find your father. Go up to **Nestor**[3] and ask him if he knows what happened to your father. He will tell you the truth, for he is an excellent person.

"Be brave. Follow what you feel, and you will do well," replied Athena.

They found Nestor with his sons. They greeted Telemachus and asked him and his crew to eat with them. Nestor said a prayer to Poseidon, the god they were honoring. "Honor him," said Nestor. "Man cannot live without the gods in the world."

After they all made an excellent dinner, Nestor again spoke: "Now," said he, "who, then, strangers, are you, and from what port have you sailed? Are you traders? Are you running away? Do you fear for your lives? Tell us your story."

Telemachus answered boldly, for Athena had given him courage. "Nestor, we come from Ithaca. I seek news of my father Odysseus. I hear he is said to have **sacked**[4] the town of Troy in your company. We have heard what happened to most of the

---

[2] **nervous**—easily excited or upset, uneasy, restless.

[3] **Nestor**—the King of Pylos.

[4] **sacked**—attacked and captured a city, taking all of the food and riches.

heroes who fought in Troy, but not of Odysseus. What do you know of him?"

"My friend," answered Nestor, "you recall a time of much sorrow. We suffered much both at sea and under Achilles. In the battle at Troy, our best men fell—Ajax, Achilles, Patroclus,[5] and my own dear son. If I talked for five years, or even six, I could not tell you all that we suffered. Nine long years we battled in Troy. During all this time no one could compare with your father, the great Odysseus.

"After those years of battle, when we set sail for home, Zeus saw fit to annoy us. Zeus's daughter, Athena, caused the trouble. A **quarrel**[6] started about when we should leave. Half of us left, and the other half—including your father Odysseus—stayed behind.

"Our trip went quickly. We offered sacrifices to Poseidon, god of the sea, and we reached our home in a short time. Therefore, my dear young friend, I returned without hearing anything about the others. I know neither who got home safely nor who was lost."

---

[5] Ajax, Achilles, and Patroclus were great warriors in the battle at Troy.

[6] **quarrel**—fight with words.

> **"A god can do anything by simply wishing it. Still, death is certain. When a man's hour is come, not even the gods can save him, no matter how fond they are of him."**

"Thank you, Nestor, for all you have told me," answered Telemachus.

"My friend," said Nestor, "I remember hearing that your mother has many uninvited suitors, who are **wrecking**[7] your estate. What do you do about this? Who knows what may happen if Odysseus comes back? He will pay these **scoundrels**[8] in full, I bet. If Athena helps you as she did Odysseus, you will defeat them. When we were fighting at Troy, I never yet saw the gods so openly fond of anyone as Athena then was of your father. She took good care of him. If she helps you as she did him, those suitors are in trouble."

Telemachus answered: "I can expect nothing of the kind."

At this, Athena said: "Telemachus, what are you talking about? A god can do anything by simply wishing it. Still, death is certain. When a man's

---

[7] **wrecking**—destroying or breaking; ruining.

[8] **scoundrels**—villains; people up to no good.

hour is come, not even the gods can save him, no matter how fond they are of him."

Telemachus answered, "Do not let us talk about it any more. There is no chance that my father is ever coming back."

"Take my **advice**,"[9] said Nestor, "and do not go traveling about for long so far from home, nor leave your property with such dangerous people in your house. They will eat up everything you have. But, having said that, I advise you by all means to go and visit **Menelaus**.[10] He is just back from a voyage among distant peoples. Go to him. Beg of him to tell you what he knows. He will tell you no lies, for he is an excellent person."

As the sun set, Athena said: "Sir, thank you for all you have told us. Let us honor **Poseidon**[11] and the other immortals and then go to bed. People should go to bed early and not keep late hours, even at a festival."

Thus spoke the daughter of Zeus, and they obeyed her. Then Athena flew away in the form of an eagle, and all marveled as they saw it. Nestor

---

[9] **advice**—an opinion about what should be done.

[10] **Menelaus**—the King of Sparta.

[11] **Poseidon**—king of the sea and brother of Zeus.

was amazed. He said to Telemachus, "My friend, I see that you are going to be a great hero some day. Already the gods are your friends. This must have been Athena, Zeus's daughter. She showed favor toward your brave father too."

They decided that Telemachus should stay there that night and in the morning take a chariot[12] to Sparta, where he would meet Menelaus. Then Telemachus got into the chariot. He whipped the horses, and they flew forward into the open country, leaving Pylos behind. Behind them the sun went down and all the roads grew dark. In the course of two days, they completed their journey and arrived in Sparta.

---

[12] **chariot**—something pulled by horses that people rode in, usually used for fighting.

BOOK IV

At Sparta, Telemachus meets Menelaus and Helen.
They tell him stories of Odysseus. Menelaus describes
his own adventures on his return from Troy. He says
the god Proteus has told him that Odysseus is a prisoner
on Calypso's isle. Back in Ithaca, the suitors plan to
murder Telemachus.

Telemachus arrived at the home of Menelaus just as the sun was setting. He found Menelaus in his house, where a double wedding feast had begun. The feast was held in honor of his son, who was getting married, and his daughter, who was going to marry the son of Achilles, the great Greek hero of the Trojan War.

A servant told Menelaus that strangers had ridden up in chariots. "Two men who look noble have just arrived. What are we to do?"

Menelaus was angry and said: "You fool. Take their horses and show the strangers in so they may join us for supper. I have often stayed at the houses of others. It is fine if they wish to stay with me."

Telemachus and Pisistratus were astonished when they saw the house of Menelaus. It was a palace, filled with riches. They looked at the fine rugs and silver plates in **awe**.[1] After-ward, the servants washed them and gave them clean shirts.

> *"Then tell us who you are. You must be sons of kings, so great do you seem."*

Then Menelaus greeted them, saying, "Please, have some supper with us. Then tell us who you are. You must be sons of kings, so great do you seem." He handed them the best pieces of meat, the part of the bull saved for the king. But Menelaus gave it to Telemachus.

As they were eating, Telemachus said to his friend, "Everything is so splendid. It is like eating in the palace of Zeus himself. I am lost in amazement."

Menelaus overheard them talking and replied: "No one, my sons, can compete with Zeus. Every-thing about him is immortal. But among men, few have more than I. I have traveled much and had

---

[1] **awe**—amazement, respect.

many adventures, and I have suffered much. I traveled for nearly eight years before I could get home with my ship. I went to Cyprus, Phoenicia, and Egypt. I went also to Arabia and Libya. But, while I was traveling, my brother was secretly murdered by a stranger. So, I have no pleasure in this wealth."

Later, Menelaus said more: "I am often sad as I sit here—sad for all of those who fought with me on the plains of Troy. At times I cry aloud in sorrow for them. Yet I also am sad for one man more than for others. I cannot even think of him without becoming miserable. No one among our soldiers risked so much or had so much courage. He has been gone so long. We know not whether he is alive or dead. He left his old father Laertes, his quiet wife Penelope, and a son called Telemachus. They are plunged into grief at what has become of him."

Thus spoke Menelaus. Then he noticed his guest was crying at these words. Tears fell from Telemachus's eyes, so Menelaus stopped. Just then the beautiful Helen, his wife, came into the hall.

"Do we know the names of these strangers, Menelaus?" she asked. "Shall I guess? Never have I seen a man so like young Odysseus. This must be Telemachus, Odysseus's son whom he left as a baby."

"My dear wife," replied Menelaus, "I see the likeness just as you do. His hands and feet are just like those of Odysseus, and so is his hair. When I was talking just now about Odysseus, saying how much he suffered, tears came from the stranger's eyes."

Telemachus's friend, Pisistratus, then said: "You are right in thinking this man is Telemachus. My own father, Nestor, sent me with him. He has had trouble at home since his father has been gone. He has no one to support him. No one stands by him, and suitors are living in his house eating everything he has."

"Bless him," Menelaus said. "I am receiving a visit from the son of my dear friend. I have wanted to repay Odysseus for all that he has done for me. I would give him a city, a palace. To Odysseus I owe so much."

Thus did Menelaus speak. His words made them all weep. Then Nestor's son Pisistratus said: "I, too, had a brother who died at Troy. You may have known him as well. His name was Antilochus. I never saw him myself, but I have heard he was brave."

"Please," Helen said, "let us hear no more sad tales. Drink some of my wine." Helen said this because she had put into the wine herbs that made those who drank it unable to be sad. Then she began her story.

"I cannot name every great deed of Odysseus. I can say what he did at Troy, for I was there. When I was held captive in the city, Odysseus covered himself with wounds and bruises. He dressed as a beggar and came into the enemy's city. No one said anything to him. I alone saw him. I washed him and put a clean **cloak**[2] around him. I promised not to tell who he was or what he had planned. Then he told of the **cunning**[3] trick he would plan. He told me of the wooden horse and how he would hide inside it with the other soldiers."

Then Menelaus said: "All that you have been saying, dear wife, is true. I have never seen another such man as Odysseus. What courage he displayed in the wooden horse. We were inside the horse, waiting to attack. Three times we heard you call out. Some god who wished to let the Trojans know we were inside tempted you to call out our names. We heard you call. Diomed and I wished to spring out at that moment and attack, but Odysseus held us back. Everyone except Anticlus was quiet. When he started to speak, Odysseus put his hand over his

---

[2] **cloak**—jacket.
[3] **cunning**—clever.

mouth. He kept Anticlus quiet until the goddess Athena took you away."

"How sad," said Telemachus, "that after all that, Odysseus was not saved." After a while, he said, "Let us sleep now. We are tired from our journey."

When dawn arose, Menelaus asked, "Why, Telemachus, did you make the long sea journey to Sparta?"

"I have come, sir, to see if you might tell me anything about my father. I am being eaten out of house and home. My fair **estate**⁴ is being wasted by men who pretend to want to marry my mother."

On hearing this, Menelaus was angry. "So," he said, "those cowards want to sleep in brave Odysseus's bed? They had better be careful. A lion that goes off to feed in the jungle comes back. And, when he does, he makes short work of them who have moved into his house."

After a few minutes, Menelaus said, "Let me tell you what I know about your father. News came from Proteus many years ago." Menelaus told a story about how he met Proteus, a sea god who lived with Poseidon. Proteus told him: "Odysseus dwells now on an island. He is very sad. He lives in

---

⁴ **estate**—property and belongings.

the house of the **nymph**[5] Calypso. She keeps him prisoner. He cannot reach his home because he has no ship and no crew."

Menelaus said to Telemachus, "I do not know where Odysseus is now. Please, stay with us ten or twelve more days."

"Do not press me to stay longer, Menelaus. I cannot stay here. If my father may live, I must find him."

Meanwhile, in Ithaca, the suitors were playing games in front of Odysseus's house. One of them asked, "When will Telemachus return? Surely he cannot be gone much longer?" They did not know yet that he had left on a voyage to find his father. "He has a ship of mine," one of them said.

"What? a ship? Why? Tell me, did you give him a ship or did he take it?"

"I gave him a ship. What else could I do when a man as great as he asks me? And, I gave him a fine crew as well."

The suitors were very angry. This voyage, they thought, was a serious matter. What if Telemachus found Odysseus? What if he found men to help

---

[5] **nymph**—a minor god in the form of a beautiful woman.

him? "We must lie in wait for him in the **straits**[6] outside Ithaca," one of the suitors said. "We will kill him before he sets foot again on this island."

Just then a servant of Penelope's came by. He overheard the suitors planning to kill Telemachus.

The servant had not told Penelope that her son had left on the voyage. Even though he was told not to say anything for twelve days, he now felt he must tell her.

> *"Dear Penelope," he said, "they are going to try to murder Telemachus when he returns from his voyage."*

"Dear Penelope," he said, "they are going to try to murder Telemachus when he returns from his voyage. He went to Pylos and Sparta to look for news of his father. But now he is in danger."

Penelope began crying. "Why did my son leave? Why did he not tell me?"

"I do not know," the servant replied. "Maybe some god sent him on this voyage. He told me not to say anything for twelve days." Penelope then left and said a prayer to the gods. She prayed to

---

[6] **straits**—narrow channels joining two larger bodies of water.

Athena. "Hear me, daughter of Zeus. Save my son. Bring my husband home. End my grief."

Athena heard Penelope's prayer. She sent a vision to Penelope. In the vision, Penelope's sister came to her. "The gods will not let you suffer. Don't be sad. Your son has not wronged the gods. He will live and come back to you."

Penelope asked about her husband Odysseus. She asked if something had happened to him. "Take heart," her sister said in the vision. "I cannot tell you whether he is alive or not."

The suitors, meanwhile, were boarding a ship to sail out to meet Telemachus when he returned to Ithaca. They had in mind to meet him at a narrow opening, where a ship can wait in **ambush**.[7] That night, in secret, they waited.

---

[7] **ambush**—attack by surprise.

BOOK V

Hermes, called by Zeus, flies to Calypso and asks her to let Odysseus go. Obeying the god, Calypso helps Odysseus to build a raft and set sail. After seventeen days of smooth sailing, his raft is wrecked in a storm made by Poseidon. Odysseus battles the waves bravely, and at last he reaches the land of the Phaeacians.

Dawn rose from her couch beside the gods and brought light for men and gods. They were all meeting with Zeus, their king. Athena began to tell them of the many sufferings of Odysseus. She asked that he be let go from the island where Calypso held him.

"Father Zeus," said Athena, "there Odysseus is, lying in great pain on Calypso's island. She will not let him go home. He cannot get back to his own country, for he can find neither ships nor sailors to take him. Plus, wicked people are now trying to murder his only son, Telemachus. He is at this moment coming home from Pylos and Sparta, where he has gone to see if he can hear news of his father."

Zeus then said to his son **Hermes,**[1] "Hermes, you are our messenger. Go tell Calypso we have decided that poor Odysseus is to return home, but only after a hard voyage of twenty days on a raft. First he is to reach the land of the Phaeacians. They will be good to him and treat him like a god. Then they will send him in a ship to his own country."

Thus Zeus spoke, and Hermes put on his glittering golden sandals and flew off. He flew and flew over many a wave in the ocean, until at last he arrived at the island. Hermes went to the cave where the nymph Calypso lived.

Hermes found her at home. There was a large fire burning, and Calypso was busy at her loom. Her home was beautiful, and even a god could not help being charmed by such a lovely spot. So Hermes stood still and looked at it, until at last he went inside her cave.

Calypso knew him at once. (The gods all know each other, no matter how far they live from one

---

[1] **Hermes**—messenger of the gods.

another.) Odysseus was not within. He was on the seashore, as usual, looking out upon the ocean. Tears filled his eyes, because his heart was breaking of sorrow.

"You ask me why I have come here," Hermes said, "and I will tell you. Zeus sent me. He says that you have here Odysseus, the most unlucky of men. He fought nine years in Troy before leaving as a hero. He sailed home in the tenth year, and, on his way home, sinned against Athena. She raised the wind and waves against him and sunk his ship. All of his brave crew died. Odysseus alone did not die. Now Zeus has said he shall go home and return to his house and country."

> **"You gods," she said, "you are always jealous. You hate seeing a goddess take a fancy to a mortal man."**

Calypso trembled with rage when she heard this. "You gods," she said, "you are always jealous. You hate seeing a goddess take a fancy to a mortal man. And now you are angry with me too because I have a man here. I found the poor creature sitting all alone on the shore. Zeus had struck his ship with lightning and sunk it in the ocean. All of Odysseus's crew were drowned. It was I who saved him and loved him. I had set my heart on making him immortal, so that he should never grow old, but I cannot cross Zeus. Yet what can I do? I cannot send Odysseus anywhere. I have neither ships nor men to take him."

"Then send him away," said Hermes, "or Zeus will be angry with you and punish you."

Calypso went out to look for Odysseus. She found him sitting on the beach, his eyes filled with tears. He was dying of homesickness. Calypso then went up close to him and said:

"My poor fellow, I am going to send you away. So go, cut some wood from my forest and make yourself a large raft. I will also give you clothes and will send you a fair wind to take you home."

Odysseus shook as he heard her. "Now, goddess," he answered, "there is something behind all this. You cannot really mean to help me home. Swear that you mean me no mischief."

Calypso smiled at this. "You know a great deal," said she, "but you are quite wrong here. My heart is not made of stone, and I am very sorry for you."

Then Odysseus and Calypso went back to her cave. After they had eaten and put on fresh clothes, Calypso said, "Odysseus, noble son of Laertes,

I wish you well. But if you could only know how much suffering is in store for you before you get back to your own country, you would stay here. Stay with me. Let me make you immortal. No matter how happy you may be to see your wife, I am surely as good-looking as she is. Is not an immortal woman much prettier than a mere mortal one?"

"Goddess," replied Odysseus, "do not be angry with me. My wife Penelope is not so beautiful as you. She is only a woman, whereas you are an immortal. Nevertheless, I want to get home and can think of nothing else. If some god wrecks me when I am on the sea, I will bear it."

> **"Nevertheless, I want to get home and can think of nothing else. If some god wrecks me when I am on the sea, I will bear it."**

In the morning, Odysseus put on his shirt and coat. Calypso gave him a great bronze ax to cut trees and build his raft. She then led the way to the far side of the island, where the tallest trees grew. By and by, Calypso brought him some cloth to make the sails. He made these too. In a few days' time he drew the raft down into the water.

It took four days to complete the work. On the fifth day, Calypso sent him from the island. Seven days later, he first saw land. It was the nearest part of the Phaeacian coast.

But King Poseidon, lord of the seas, caught sight of Odysseus a long way off. Poseidon could see him sailing upon the sea, and it made him very angry. Poseidon shook his head and muttered to himself, saying, "So the gods have been changing their minds about Odysseus. They never told me about it. Still, I can make his ride rough."

Then he gathered his clouds together, grasped his **trident**,[2] and stirred it round in the sea. Winds from the east, south, north, and west fell upon Odysseus all at the same time. A tremendous sea arose, and Odysseus's raft began to turn over.

"Alas," he said to himself, "what will become of me? I am afraid Calypso was right. I should have trouble at sea before I get back home. What she said is now all coming true."

As he spoke, the sea broke over him with terrific fury, and he was carried overboard. Odysseus swam in the storm for a long time. Many times he went under the waves. His clothes pulled him down, and he nearly drowned. At last he climbed on one part from his raft.

---

[2] **trident**—the three-pronged spear carried by Poseidon.

Poseidon watched him as he did so. Poseidon wagged his head, saying, "There now, swim up and down as best you can. I do not think you will be able to say that I have let you off too lightly."

But Athena came to help Odysseus. She stopped most of the winds and pushed Odysseus toward the land of the Phaeacians, where he would be safe.

Odysseus had floated for two nights and two days in the water. On the third day, Odysseus at last set foot upon dry ground. As he did so, he said a prayer to Zeus: "Hear me, O king, and save me from the anger of the sea-god Poseidon. Have mercy upon me, O king, for I declare myself your servant."

In the end, Odysseus found some high ground not far from the water. There he crawled under two olive trees. He began to make himself a bed of leaves on which to lie. Then, alone in a faraway country, far from friends and family, Odysseus looked up at the skies. Athena then came to him. She placed a sweet sleep upon his eyes and made him forget his sorrows.

BOOK VI

Nausicaa, daughter of King Alcinous of the Phaeacians, goes to the ocean to do washing. She sees Odysseus, and he asks for her help. She gives him food and invites him to her father's house.

So here Odysseus slept on the beach, under some trees. Meanwhile Athena went off to the city of the Phaeacians, where King Alcinous ruled. Athena went straight to the bedroom of a girl as lovely as a goddess, Nausicaa, the daughter of King Alcinous. She was sleeping, and Athena came to her in her dreams. Athena took the form of the daughter of a famous sea captain, who was a dear friend of Nausicaa. She said, "Nausicaa, what can your mother have been thinking about to have such a lazy daughter? Here are your clothes lying all about. Suppose we wash them tomorrow. Gather them up. Ask your father for a wagon and some mules for tomorrow. They will help us carry the rugs, robes, and **girdles**[1] to the washing place."

After she said this, Athena went off to Olympus, home of the gods. By and by, Nausicaa awoke. She began to wonder about her dream and went to tell her father and mother about it.

"Papa dear, could you let me use the big wagon? I want to take all of our dirty clothes to the ocean and wash them. You should have a clean shirt, and so should your five sons. They are all good-looking young men and should have clean clothes when they go to the dance."

"You shall have your mules, my love, and whatever else you want. Be off. The men will get you a strong wagon that will hold all of your clothes."

Nausicaa's mother prepared a basket with food and a **goatskin**[2] of wine. She also gave her a jar of oil, for softening the girls' skins after bathing. Then Nausicaa and her maids set off.

When they reached the washing pools, they took the clothes out of the wagon, put them in the water, and began washing them. It took most of the day. Then they laid the clothes out by the seaside to

---

[1] **girdles**—belts or sashes worn around the waist.
[2] **goatskin**—container made from the skin of a goat.

dry. Afterward they started washing and **anointing**[3] themselves with the oil and preparing dinner. After dinner, they began to play ball, and Nausicaa sang for them.

When it was time to start home, Athena decided that Odysseus should wake up and see this handsome girl. Athena then threw the ball at one of the maids but missed her, so that it went far off into the water. At this, they shouted. The noise they made awoke Odysseus, who was sleeping after being shipwrecked on his voyage.

"Alas," he said to himself, "what sort of people have I come upon? I hear the voices of young women. They sound like nymphs that live in the mountaintops. Let me see if I can get a look at them."

As he said this, he came out from under the bush where he was sleeping. He broke off a branch from a tree to cover his nakedness. He looked like some wild animal, with salt covering his beard.

On seeing him, the maids ran off, but Nausicaa stood firm, right in front of Odysseus.

"O, queen," he said, "I beg for your help. Are you a goddess or a mortal woman? If you are a

---

[3] **anointing**—to put oil on, for smoothing skin or as part of a religious ceremony.

goddess, I can only believe you are Zeus's daughter. But, if you are mortal, what happiness you must bring your family.

"I am in bad shape. For twenty days I have been tossing upon the sea in storms. The winds have taken me all the way from Calypso's island to here. Pity me, O queen. You are the first person I have met in this country. Please, let me have something to cover myself and some food."

To this Nausicaa answered, "Stranger, Zeus treats people as he likes, and there is no telling how he chooses to treat people. Make the best of what he gives you. Now that you have come to our country, you shall not want for clothes or food.

"I shall show you the way into town. We are the Phaeacians. I am the daughter of King Alcinous." And then, to her maids, Nausicaa shouted: "Stay where you are. Do you take this man for a robber or murderer? Look, he is only a poor man who has lost his way. We must be kind to him. So, girls, give him something to eat and drink and then wash him."

> **"I am in bad shape. For twenty days I have been tossing upon the sea in storms. The winds have taken me all the way from Calypso's island to here."**

At this the maids brought Odysseus a shirt and cloak. But he said, "Young women, please, keep away a little and let me wash the salt from my shoulders. I will put the oil on myself. Besides, I am ashamed to strip before all you good-looking women."

When Odysseus had washed himself, he put oil over his body and put on the clothes given to him. Athena made him look taller and stronger than before. She also made his hair grow thicker. So, when he went off by the beach, he looked quite young and handsome.

Nausicaa looked at him with admiration. "My dears," she said to her maids, "I think the gods have sent this man to my people. When I first saw him, he looked plain. But now he looks like one of the gods who dwell in heaven. I should like my future husband to be just like him. Give him something to eat and drink."

Odysseus ate and drank like a man who hadn't eaten in months. "Stranger," Nausicaa said, "come and let us go back into town. I will introduce you to my father. But, stay behind the wagon with the maids. Then, when we get near the town, go off around the wall. Come in the back way, so people will not talk about the strange man who joined us."

So saying, Nausicaa lashed the mules and started off. Odysseus took a moment to pray to the gods. "Hear me, daughter of Zeus, for you paid no attention to me when Poseidon was wrecking my ship with waves. Have pity upon me. Grant that I may find friends here and be well received by these people."

Athena heard his prayer, but she did not show herself to him openly. She was afraid of her uncle Poseidon, who was still furious at Odysseus.

BOOK VII

Athena shows Odysseus to the palace of King Alcinous and Queen Arete. They welcome him and listen while he explains how he landed on their shores. Moved by his tale, they promise to send him safely back to his home.

Odysseus waited and prayed outside town. Nausicaa went on into town on her own. After a while, Odysseus went into town. The goddess Athena again came to help him. She spread a mist around Odysseus, so no one would see him.

Then, after he was within the walls of the town, Athena, now looking like a little girl carrying a pitcher, came up to him. She stood right in front of him, and Odysseus said:

"Little one, will you be so kind as to show me the house of King Alcinous? I am lost and do not know anyone in your town and country."

Then Athena said, "I will show you the house you want. Alcinous lives near to my own house. But do not say a word as you go. Do not look at any man, or ask him questions. The people here do not like men who come from other places."

Athena led the way, and Odysseus followed in her steps. But no one could see him as he passed through the city because of the mist. Odysseus admired the harbors, ships, and high walls of the city. When they reached the king's house, Athena said:

"This is the house that you would have me show you. You will find a number of great people sitting at the table, but do not be afraid. Go straight in, for the bolder a man is, the more likely he is to be heard, even though he is a stranger. First find the queen. Her name is Arete. She comes of the same people as her husband Alcinous. They both are related to Poseidon.

"Arete is greatly respected by everyone, for she is a thoroughly good woman both in head and heart. If you can gain her goodwill, you will see your friends again and get safely back to your country."

Then Athena left and went away over the sea. Odysseus went on to the house of Alcinous. The palace was so beautiful he could not believe his eyes. The doors were gold and hung on **pillars**[1] of silver.

Odysseus stood for a while and looked about him before entering the house of Alcinous. There he found all the chief people among the Phaeacians. He went straight to Arete and King Alcinous. The cloud of mist still covered him, so no one could see him. Then he laid his hands upon the knees of the queen. At that moment, the mist fell away from him, and he became **visible**.[2] Everyone was speechless with surprise. But Odysseus began at once:

> *"Queen Arete," he said, "help get me home to my own country as soon as possible. I have been long in trouble and away from my friends."*

"Queen Arete," he said, "help me get home to my own country as soon as possible. I have been long in trouble and away from my friends."

Then Odysseus sat down by the fireside. At first, everyone was quiet. Then the old hero Echeneus, the oldest of the Phaeacians, said:

"Alcinous, who is this stranger? Where did he come from? Quick, give him something to eat and drink. Then tell us about him."

---

[1] **pillars**—vertical columns used to support a building or structure.

[2] **visible**—able to be seen.

Alcinous took Odysseus by the hand and showed him to a seat next to him. It was a place of honor. They brought him water in a beautiful golden basin[3] for him to wash his hands. Then they brought him food and drink.

Odysseus ate and drank with thanks. Then Alcinous said to one of the servants, "Mix a cup of wine and hand it round that we may drink offerings to Zeus.

"Now you have had your supper, go to bed. Tomorrow morning I shall invite a still larger number of people here. We will have a meal in your honor. We will talk then about how we may send you back rejoicing to your own country, no matter how distant it may be. We must see that you come to no harm while on your journey.

"Pray, Alcinous, do not think such things. I have nothing of the immortal about me, neither in body nor mind."

"It is possible that you are one of the immortals who has come down from heaven to visit us."

Then Odysseus said: "Pray, Alcinous, do not think such things. I have nothing of the immortal about me, neither in body nor mind.

---

[3] **basin**—large bowl.

Let me eat in spite of sorrow, for I have an empty stomach. I am in great trouble, but I need to eat and drink now. Let me lay aside all memory of my sorrows."

After Odysseus spoke, everyone went home to bed. Odysseus was left in the courtyard with Arete and Alcinous. Arete was the first to speak. She saw the shirt, cloak, and clothes that Odysseus was wearing. They were her work and that of her maids. So she said, "Stranger, before we go any further, there is a question I should like to ask you. Who gave you those clothes?"

And Odysseus answered: "It would be a long story if I told you all of my sorrows. But, about your question, there is an island far away called Ogygian. Here dwells the powerful goddess Calypso. She lives by herself. Zeus struck my ship with his thunderbolts and broke it up in mid-ocean. Every man on my ship drowned, but I was carried for nine days. On the tenth night, the gods brought me to where the great goddess Calypso lives. She took me in and treated me with the utmost kindness. Indeed, she wanted to make me immortal that I might never grow old.

"I stayed with Calypso seven years. In the eighth year, she let me leave of my own free will. Zeus told her she must let me go, or she changed her mind. She sent me from her island on a raft. I sailed at sea on the raft for many days. Suddenly, a great storm came up. The sea was so terribly high that I could no longer stay on my raft. Finally, I had to swim for my life, and that is how I came to your shores.

"Sick and sorry, I slept among the leaves all the first night I landed here. When I woke, I saw your daughter's servants playing upon the beach. Your daughter helped me. She gave me plenty of bread and wine. She washed me in the river and gave me the clothes in which you see me. These are the facts."

Then Alcinous said, "Stranger, it was wrong of my daughter not to bring you at once to my house."

Replied Odysseus, "She is not to blame. She did tell me to follow her here, but I was ashamed and afraid. I thought you might not like me if you saw me. Every human is afraid sometimes."

"Stranger," replied Alcinous, "I am not the kind of man to be angry about nothing. Now that I see what kind of person you are, I wish you would stay here. Marry my daughter, and become my son-in-law. If you stay, I will give you a house. But no one will keep you here against your own will. You may be sure of that.

"Or if you wish, my sailors will take you to your home. You will see what fine sailors I have. You may even sleep the entire way to your home, if you wish."

Odysseus prayed aloud, saying, "Father Zeus, grant that Alcinous may do all as he has said. If he does, he will become famous, and I shall return to my own country."

Then Arete told her maids to set a bed in the room that was in the gatehouse. The maids went out with torches in their hands. When they had made the bed, they came to Odysseus and said, "Rise, sir stranger, and come with us, for your bed is ready."

So Odysseus slept in a warm bed placed in a safe room, dreaming of going home.

BOOK VIII

The next day King Alcinous orders a ship made ready for Odysseus. He gives a large banquet for the Phaeacians. They have athletic contests, and the chiefs give many gifts to Odysseus. Then the king begs Odysseus to tell who he is and where he came from.

Alcinous led the way to the palace. Athena took the form of one of Alcinous's servants. She went to the citizens and said: "Come to the gathering, all of you, and listen to the stranger who has just come off a long voyage to the house of King Alcinous. He looks like a god."

With these words, she made them all want to come to the gathering at the palace. Everyone was struck with the way Odysseus looked. Athena had made him look taller and more handsome. She wanted everyone to know what a great man Odysseus was.

"Hear me," said Alcinous. "This stranger has found his way to my house. I still don't know his name. He wants to go home and wishes us to help him. Let us pull a ship into the sea with fifty of our best young sailors. Then, when the ship is ready, come to my house for a feast."

Alcinous then led the way, and the others followed. They got the ship ready. Then they came on shore and went to the house of King Alcinous. He killed a dozen sheep, eight full-grown pigs, and two oxen. These were skinned and cooked for a great feast.

The company then ate and drank the good things before them. Afterward, the poet Demodocus sang about the great heroes and the fight between Odysseus and Achilles years ago during the Trojan War.

As Demodocus sang, Odysseus drew his purple cape over his head and covered his face. He was ashamed to let the Phaeacians see him crying. He wiped the tears from his eyes, uncovered his face, and drank to their health. No one noticed Odysseus crying except Alcinous. He was sitting nearby and heard the heavy sighs. So he said, "We have had enough now. Let us begin the sports, so that our guest can return home to tell others how great a people we are."

The foot races came first. The runners raised a dust upon the plain as they all ran off at the same moment. Next they turned to wrestling and jumping.

Alcinous's son Laodamas was the best boxer. He was the one who said, "Let us ask the stranger whether he is good at any of these sports. He is not old, and he seems very powerfully built: his thighs, calves, hands, and neck are large. But he has suffered much lately, and there is nothing like the sea for wearing out a man, no matter how strong he is."

So he said to Odysseus, "I hope, sir, that you will enter one of our games. Show us what you've got. You will return home soon. The ship is all ready and the crew is chosen."

Odysseus answered, "Laodamas, why do you tempt me in this way? I am thinking of going home, not contests. I have been through much trouble."

Then Seareach, son of a sailor, said: "I gather, then, that you are not much of an athlete."

"For shame, sir!" answered Odysseus, fiercely. "You are quite mistaken, for I do well in a great many sports."

So Odysseus, without even taking his shirt off, seized a **discus**.[1] It was larger and much heavier than those used by the Phaeacians. Then, swinging it back, Odysseus threw it the farthest anyone had yet thrown. Athena, now in the form of a man, came and marked the place where it had fallen. "A blind man, sir," said Athena, "could easily see no one else has thrown it this far."

Odysseus was glad that he had found a friend among the crowd. "Young men," said he, "come up and outthrow that if you can. I will box, wrestle, or run. I do not care what it is.

"I am a good hand at every kind of athletic sport. In battle I am always the first to bring a man down with my arrow. **Philoctetes**[2] was the only man who could shoot better than I could at Troy. I can throw a dart farther than anyone else can shoot an arrow. Running is the only sport at which I am not very good. I am still weak from having been at sea so long."

"I am a good hand at every kind of athletic sport. In battle I am always the first to bring a man down with my arrow. Philoctetes was the only man who could shoot better than I could at Troy."

---

[1] **discus**—circular, flat object that is thrown for distance in athletic games.
[2] **Philoctetes**—a skilled archer who fought with the Greeks at Troy.

They all held their peace except King Alcinous. He said: "Sir, I understand that you are willing to show your strength. The remarks of the other athletes probably insulted you. As a people, we are not particularly remarkable for our boxing, nor yet as wrestlers. But we are good runners and excellent sailors. We also like good dinners, music, and dancing. So now, please, enjoy some of our best dancers."

The dancing went on for a long time. Odysseus said: "King Alcinous, you said your people were the best dancers in the world, and tonight they have proved that. I was astonished at what I saw."

The king was delighted at this. He then exclaimed to the Phaeacians: "Good people, each of you, give Odysseus a clean coat, a shirt, and a fine gold coin. Then he will leave our dinner and our land happy."

Then the man called Seareach said: "King Alcinous, I will give the stranger my sword, which is made of bronze and silver. It will be worth a great deal to him."

As he spoke, he placed the sword in the hands of Odysseus. Seareach said to him: "Good luck to you, stranger. May heaven grant you a safe return. I understand you have been away a long time and have gone through much hardship."

To which Odysseus answered: "Good luck to you too, my friend. May the gods grant you every happiness. I hope you will not miss the sword you have given me."

"Wife," said Alcinous, turning to Queen Arete, "go, get the best chest we have, and put a clean cloak and shirt in it. Also, warm some water over the fire. Let our guest take a warm bath. See also to the careful packing of all of his presents. I shall give him this golden cup. I hope it reminds him of us for the rest of his life whenever he drinks from it."

Then Arete told her maids to set a large pot on the fire, and they thus warmed the bathwater. Meanwhile, Arete brought a **magnificent**[3] chest from her own room. Inside it she packed all the beautiful presents her people had brought. Last, she added a cloak and a good shirt from Alcinous.

Odysseus was very glad to have a warm bath. When the servants were done washing and anointing him with oil and had given him a clean

---

[3] **magnificent**—beautiful, stunning.

cloak and shirt, he joined the other guests. Lovely Nausicaa admired him as she saw him pass. "Farewell, stranger," said she, "do not forget me when you are safe at home again. Remember, I saved your life."

And Odysseus said, "Nausicaa, daughter of great Alcinous, may Zeus, the mighty husband of Hera, grant that I may reach my home. I also ask that he bless you as my guardian angel all my days, for it was you who saved me."

After he had said this, Odysseus seated himself beside Alcinous. Supper was then served. A servant led in the blind poet Demodocus and set him in the company. Demodocus sang of Odysseus and the fall of Troy. No one yet knew that the stranger among them was Odysseus!

Then Alcinous, who saw Odysseus weeping, said, "During our feast, since our fine poet sang, our guest has been unhappy. Now, friend, tell me the name by which your father and mother used to call you. Tell me also your country, nation, and city, that our ships may take you there."

Odysseus was quiet for a moment. "And now," continued Alcinous, "tell me and tell me true. Where have you been wandering, and in what countries have you traveled? Tell us of the peoples themselves, and of their cities. Who were savage? Who were kind? Tell us also why you are so unhappy when Demodocus sings of the heroes of Troy. Did you lose a brave friend there? Tell us what happened to you."

BOOK IX

Odysseus now tells his name. He begins the long story of his adventures since leaving Troy. With twelve ships he sailed first to Ismarus. There he sacked a city. Then he was driven by storms to the land of the Lotus-eaters. Odysseus next sailed to the land of the Cyclops. There he was trapped in the cave of the monster Polyphemus. Odysseus and a few of his men escaped, but many others were killed.

Odysseus answered, "King Alcinous, it is wonderful to hear a singer with such a beautiful voice. Now, since you ask the story of my sorrows, I will tell you.

"First, I will tell you my name. I am Odysseus, son of Laertes. I live in Ithaca. Now I will tell you of the many dangerous adventures I had on my return from Troy.

"I sailed first to Ismarus, which is the city of Cicones. There I looted the town and attacked the people. We took their wives and much booty. I then said that we had better leave at once. But my men would not obey me. They stayed there drinking wine and killing many sheep and oxen. Meanwhile the Cicones cried out for help from other Cicones who lived inland. In the morning, they attacked us in large numbers. By sundown, we had lost six men from every ship we had. We got away with the men who were left.

"We sailed onward with sorrow in our hearts. Then Zeus raised the north wind against us till it blew a hurricane. The wind tore our sails to shreds, so we took them down. We rowed our hardest toward the land. There we lay two days and two nights. On the morning of the third day, we again set sail.

"We were driven off course by strong winds for nine days. On the tenth day we reached the land of the Lotus-eaters. They live on a food that comes from a kind of flower. We landed there to find fresh water, and we ate our lunch on the shore.

"When we landed, I sent three men to see what kind of people they were. The Lotus-eaters did them no harm, but gave them the lotus to eat.

Those who ate it lost all memory of home and duty and wanted to stay there forever, munching lotus with the Lotus-eaters. But I forced them back to the ships, although they wept bitterly.

"We sailed away until we came to the land of the lawless and inhuman Cyclops, a wild race of one-eyed giants. The Cyclops do not plant or plow. They live on wheat, barley, and wild grapes. They live in caves on the tops of high mountains. Each is lord and master in his own family. They pay no attention to their neighbors.

"There is a wooded and fertile island not far off. It has no living thing upon it except wild goats.

"We entered the harbor. When we had **beached**[1] the ships, we went ashore and camped on the beach till daybreak.

"When the morning came, we got our spears and bows and arrows from the ships. We began to shoot the goats with great success. We ate and drank our fill, then camped down on the beach. Next morning, I called the men together.

"'Stay here, my brave fellows,' said I. 'I will go with my ship and its crew and explore these people

---

[1] **beached**—run ashore.

myself. I want to see if they are uncivilized savages, or a **hospitable**[2] and kind race!'

"When we got to the land, we saw a great cave overhung with bushes. This was the home of a huge Cyclops named Polyphemus, who led the life of an outlaw. He was a horrid creature, not like a human being at all. He was a giant and lived alone.

"I told my men to draw the ship ashore, and stay where they were. I took the twelve best men and a supply of food with me.

"We soon reached the monster's cave, but he was out **shepherding**.[3] We went inside and looked around. His cheese-racks were loaded with cheeses. He had more lambs and **kids**[4] than his **pens**[5] could hold. All the bowls and milk pails in his dairy were filled with **whey**.[6] My men begged me to let them steal some cheese and take it to the ship. They would then return, drive down the lamb and kids, put them on board, and sail away. But I would not listen to them. I wanted to see the owner himself.

---

[2] **hospitable**—treating guests warmly and generously.

[3] **shepherding**—taking care of sheep.

[4] **kids**—young goats.

[5] **pens**—fenced-in areas.

[6] **whey**—the watery part of milk that separates from the curds, as in the process of making cheese.

"When he finally came, he brought with him a huge load of dry firewood to light the fire for his supper. He drove all the **ewes**[7] inside, as well as the she-goats that he was going to milk. Then he rolled a huge stone to the mouth of the cave. The stone was so huge that two and twenty strong four-wheeled wagons would not have been enough to move it from the doorway. After this, he sat down and milked his ewes and goats. When he was through with all his work, he lit the fire and then caught sight of us.

"'Strangers, who are you?' he asked. 'Where do you sail from?'

"We were frightened by his loud voice and **monstrous**[8] form. But I managed to say, 'We are Achaeans on our way home from Troy. Storms have driven us far off our course. We ask you to show us some hospitality and give us such presents as visitors may reasonably expect.

"To this he answered: 'Stranger, you are a fool, or else you know nothing of this country. We Cyclops do not care about Zeus or any of your blessed gods. We are much stronger than they are. And now tell me where you tied your ship when you came on shore.'

---

[7] **ewes**—female sheep.

[8] **monstrous**—very large, enormous.

"I answered with a lie. 'Poseidon sent my ship on the rocks at the far end of your country and wrecked it. I and those with me escaped the jaws of death.'

"The cruel monster gave me no answer. But he suddenly grabbed two of my men and threw them down upon the ground. Then he tore them apart and gobbled them up like a lion in the wilderness. When the Cyclops had filled his huge stomach, he stretched himself full-length upon the ground and went to sleep. I was tempted to stab him to death with my sword. But I knew we couldn't move the stone from in front of the door. We would be trapped inside. So we stayed, sobbing and sighing where we were till morning came.

"At dawn the Cyclops again lit his fire and milked his goats and ewes. Then he grabbed two more of my men and began eating them for his morning's meal. Soon after, he rolled the stone away from the door and drove out his sheep. But he at once put it back again.

"I decided upon the following plan. The Cyclops had a large club, which was lying near one of the sheep pens. I cut off about six feet of the club and shaped it to a point. Then I hid the club. I told the men to decide which of them should help me drive it into the monster's eye while he was asleep. In the evening the monster drove his **flocks**[9] into the cave, and this time did not leave any outside. As soon as he had put the stone back in its place against the door, he sat down and milked his ewes and his goats. Then he grabbed two more of my men and made his supper from them. I went up to him with a cup of black wine in my hands, wine that I had brought with me. This wine was extremely strong, and I had been saving it for an occasion like this.

"'Look here, Cyclops,' said I, 'you have been eating a great deal of man's flesh. Take this and drink some wine. I was bringing it to you in the hope that you would take pity upon me and help me get home.'

"He then took the cup and drank. He was delighted with the taste and begged for more. 'Please, tell me your name at once,' he said, 'I want to give you a present.'

"I filled the cup for him three times and three times he drank it. When I saw that the wine had gone to his head and that he was confused, I said to

---

[9] **flocks**—groups of animals that feed together.

him: 'Cyclops, you ask my name and I will tell you. Give me the present you promised me. My name is No Man. This is what my father and mother and friends have always called me.'

"But the monster said, 'Then I will eat all No man's companions before No Man himself. I will keep No Man for the last. This is the present that I will make him.'

"As he spoke, he fell to the ground. The wine had made him drunk. From his mouth, he dribbled streams of wine and bits of men. A deep sleep took hold of him. Then I stuck the beam of wood far into the fire. When the wood was about to blaze, I pulled it out of the fire.

Then, in one great thrust, we shoved the sharp end of the beam into the monster's only eye. The boiling blood bubbled all over it as we twisted it round and round. The steam from the burning eyeball burned his eyelids and eyelashes. His yells made the cave ring. We ran away in fear. He pulled the beam from his eye and threw it in a fit of rage and pain. He shouted to the other Cyclops who lived nearby. They came out of their caves from all

" 'Then I will eat all No Man's companions before No Man himself. I will keep No Man for the last. This is the present that I will make him.' "

around and called out to ask what was the matter with him.

"'Why is it, Polyphemus,' said they, for that was the name of the Cyclops, 'that you make such a noise and keep us from sleeping? Surely No Man is carrying off your sheep? Surely No Man is trying to kill you either by tricks or by force?'

"Polyphemus shouted to them: 'No Man is killing me! No Man is killing me by force!'

"'Then,' said they, 'if no man is attacking you, you must be sick. When Zeus makes people sick, there is no help for it. You had better pray to your father Poseidon.'

"They went back into the caves. I laughed at the success of my clever plan. But Cyclops, groaning in pain, felt about with his hands till he found the stone and took it from the door. In the morning he sat in the doorway and stretched his hands in front of it to catch anyone going out with the sheep.

"That day I kept trying to think how I could save my own life and those of my companions. I decided on the following plan. I tied the **rams**[10] in threes together, with some of the twigs that

---

[10] **rams**—male sheep.

Polyphemus used to sleep on. My plan was to tie three sheep together and put a man under the middle sheep. The two on either side were to shield him. There was one ram finer than any of the others. I caught hold of him by the back and buried myself in the thick wool under his belly. I hung on patiently to his **fleece**,[11] face upward, keeping a firm hold on it all the time.

"Then we waited in great fear till morning came. When dawn appeared, the male sheep hurried out to feed. The ewes remained in their pens waiting to be milked. Their master, in spite of all his pain, felt the backs of all the sheep. He did not realize that all my men were underneath their bellies. As my ram was going out, last of all, Polyphemus grabbed it and said:

"'My good ram, what is it that makes you the last to leave my cave this morning? You do not usually let the others go out before you. Is it because you know your master has lost his eye? Are you sad because the wicked No Man and his men have gotten him drunk and blinded him? I will kill him yet.'

"As he spoke, he drove the ram outside. When we were a little way out from the cave, I got out from under the ram's belly. Then I freed my men. We managed to drive the sheep down to the ship,

---

[11] **fleece**—the wool of a sheep.

where the crew rejoiced at seeing those of us who had escaped death. They wept for the others whom the Cyclops had killed. I told them to hush their crying and get all the sheep on board at once. We then sailed out to sea. When I had got as far out as my voice would reach, I began to insult the Cyclops.

"'Cyclops,' said I, 'you should have thought before eating up my companions in your cave. Now Zeus and the other gods have punished you.'

"He became more and more furious as he heard me. He tore the top off of a high mountain and threw it in front of my ship. The wave caused by this forced us back toward the shore. I told my men that they must row for their lives. When we had gotten twice as far as we were before, I shouted out to him in my anger, 'Cyclops, if anyone asks you who it was that put out your eye, say it was the brave warrior Odysseus.'

"He groaned and called out, 'Alas, the old **prophecy**[12] about me is coming true. There was a prophet here at one time named Telemus. He told me that I would lose my sight by the hand of Odysseus. Come here, then, Odysseus, so I may give you presents. I will tell Poseidon to help you

---

[12] **prophecy**—prediction of the future.

on your journey. Poseidon and I are father and son. He alone has the power to heal me.'

"Then I said, 'It will take more than Poseidon to cure that eye of yours.'

"On this, he lifted up his hands to heaven and prayed, 'Hear me, great Poseidon! If I am indeed your own son, see that Odysseus never reaches his home alive. Or if he must get back to his home, let him do so only after losing all his men. Let him reach his home in another man's ship and find trouble in his house.'

"Poseidon heard his prayer. Then Cyclops picked up a rock much larger than the first and threw it toward our ship. The wave it raised pushed us again toward the shore of the island, where our men awaited our return.

"We ran our ship upon the sands and got out. We also landed the Cyclops's sheep and divided them equally among us. I sacrificed the ram on the seashore and offered it to Zeus, who is the lord

"'Hear me, great Poseidon! If I am indeed your own son, see that Odysseus never reaches his home alive. Or if he must get back to his home, let him do so only after losing all his men. Let him reach his home in another man's ship and find trouble in his house.'"

of all. But Zeus paid no attention to my sacrifice. He thought only of how he might destroy my ship and my companions.

"We ate our fill of meat and drink, then camped upon the beach. When dawn appeared, I told my men to go on board and loose the ropes. We sailed on with sorrow in our hearts, having our precious lives, but not our dear friends."

BOOK X

Odysseus and his ships came next to the isle of Aeolus. Aeolus gave Odysseus a bag of winds to hold tight until he reached home. But while he slept, his men opened the bag, allowing the winds to escape. The ships were blown to the land of the savage Laestrygonians, who sank eleven of their ships and ate their crews. Odysseus sought shelter on Circe's isle. Here, half of his men drank Circe's magic potion and were changed into pigs. Odysseus convinced Circe to restore them to human shape. They stayed feasting with her for a year. Then they left for Hades.

"We then went on to the island where **Aeolus**[1] lived. Aeolus had six daughters and six strong sons. They all lived with their dear father and mother, enjoying every kind of luxury. All day long the house was filled with the smell of roasting meats.

---

[1] **Aeolus**—god of the wind.

"Zeus had made Aeolus captain over the winds. He could stir or still each one of them according to his own pleasure. So he skinned an ox hide to hold the roaring winds, which he shut up in the hide as in a sack. He put the sack in the ship and tied it tightly with a silver thread.

"Nine days and nine nights did we sail. On the tenth day our homeland showed on the **horizon**.[2] I was very tired and fell into a light sleep. While I slept, the men began talking among themselves. They said I was bringing back gold and silver in the sack that Aeolus had given me. 'Bless my heart,' one would say, 'how this man is honored. He makes friends wherever we go. See what fine prizes he is taking home from Troy, yet we come back empty-handed. And now Aeolus has given him even more. Quick, let us see how much gold and silver is in the sack.'

"They opened the sack, and the winds flew howling out and raised a storm that carried us far away from our own country. Then I awoke. I did not know whether to throw myself into the sea or to live on and make the best of it. I covered

---

[2] **horizon**—place where the land appears to meet the sky.

myself up and lay down in the ship, while the men complained.

"We reached the Aeolian island again and went ashore. After dinner, I took a group of my men and went straight to the house of Aeolus. We found him feasting with his wife and family. They were shocked when they saw us and said, 'Odysseus, what brings you here? What god has been treating you so badly? We took great pains to help you on your way home to Ithaca.'

" 'Evil man, leave this island at once. I will help no one whom heaven hates.' "

"I spoke as movingly as I could, but Aeolus answered, 'Evil man, leave this island at once. I will help no one whom heaven hates.' With these words he sent me from his door.

"We sailed on sadly till the men were worn out with rowing, for there was no longer any wind to help them. Six days and nights we struggled. On the seventh day we reached the city of Laestrygonians.

"We found the harbor entirely surrounded by land under steep cliffs, with a narrow entrance between two **headlands**.³ My captains took all their

---

³ **headlands**—a point of land, usually high with a steep drop, extending out into a body of water.

ships inside and tied them tightly to one another. I kept my own ship outside and tied it to a rock at the very end of the point. I climbed a high rock but could see no sign of man or cattle, only some smoke rising in the distance. So I sent three of my men to find out what sort of people lived here.

"The men followed a level road until they met a young woman who had come outside to get water. She was daughter to a Laestrygonian named Antiphates. They asked her who the king of that country was and what kind of people he ruled. So she directed them to her father's house. When they got there, they found his wife to be a giantess as huge as a mountain. They were horrified at the sight of her.

"She at once called her husband Antiphates, who immediately began killing my men. He snatched up one of them and began to make his dinner of him. The other two ran back to the ships as fast as they could. But Antiphates called out and thousands of sturdy Laestrygonians speared them like fishes and took them home to eat. While they were killing my men within the harbor, I cut the cable of my own ship and told my men to row with all their might. We were thankful when we got into the open water, out of the reach of the rocks they hurled at us. As for the others, not one of them was left.

"Then we sailed on until we came to the island where Circe lives. She is a great and clever goddess. We brought our ship into a safe harbor. We lay there for two days and two nights, worn out in body and mind. On the morning of the third day, I went away from the ship to explore. Climbing to the top of a high lookout, I saw smoke rising from Circe's house. I decided to go back to the ship, give the men their dinners, and send some of them instead of going myself.

"When I had nearly gotten back to the ship, some god took pity upon me and sent a fine **stag**[4] right into my path. As he passed, I struck him in the middle of the back with the bronze point of my spear. It went right through him. He lay groaning in the dust until the life went out of him. I gathered rough grass and plants and twisted them into a good, stout rope. I tied the four feet of the creature together, then hung him round my neck and walked back to the ship.

"I called the men and said cheerfully, 'Look here, friends, we are not going to die before

---

[4] **stag**—adult male deer.

our time after all. We will not starve, for we have something to eat and drink on board.' They feasted their eyes upon the stag, then washed their hands, and began to cook him for dinner.

"We ate and drank our fill, then camped upon the seashore for the night. When dawn came, I called a meeting and said, 'My friends, we are in a tough spot. We have no idea where the sun either sets or rises, so that we do not even know east from west. We are certainly on an island, for I went as high as I could this morning and saw the sea reaching all round it to the horizon. Toward the middle of the island, I saw smoke rising from out of a thick forest of trees.'

"I divided them into two companies and set a captain over each. I gave one company to Eurylochus, the husband of my sister and one of my best sailors, while I took command of the other myself. Then we cast lots in a helmet, and the job of checking out Circe's house fell upon Eurylochus. He set out with twenty-two of his men.

"When they reached Circe's house, they found wild mountain wolves and lions prowling all round it. They were poor creatures whom she had tamed by her magic spells and drugged. They were totally under her power. They did not attack my men; instead, they rubbed their noses lovingly against them. My men reached the gates of the goddess's house. They could hear Circe within, singing as she worked at her loom. Polites, whom I valued and trusted more than any other of my men, said, 'There is someone inside working at a loom and singing beautifully. Let us call her and see whether she is woman or goddess.'

"They called her, and she opened the door and asked them to enter. Eurylochus, who suspected trouble, stayed outside. Circe made a mix of cheese, honey, and wine for the men, but she drugged the mix with wicked poisons to make the men forget their homes. When they had drunk the mix, she flew after them with her long stick, turned them into pigs, and shut them up in her pen. They were like pigs—head, hair, and all, and they grunted just as pigs do. But their senses were the same as before, and they remembered everything.

"When they had drunk the mix, she flew after them with her long stick, turned them into pigs, and shut them up in her pen. They were like pigs—head, hair, and all, and they grunted just as pigs do."

"Eurylochus hurried back to tell me what had happened to our men. He tried to speak but his eyes filled with tears, and he could only sob and sigh. At last we forced his story out of him, and he told us what had happened.

"Upon hearing of Circe's evil deed, I took my sword and slung it over my shoulders. I told Eurylochus to come with me and show me the way. But he laid hold of me with both hands and pleaded, 'Sir, do not force me to go with you. I know you will not bring one of them back with you. You will not return alive yourself. Let us see if we can escape with the few of us that are left. We may still save our lives.'

"'Stay where you are, then,' I answered, 'but I must go, for it is my duty.'

"So with this I left the ship and went to the house of Circe. There I met Hermes, the gods' messenger, with his golden **wand**,[5] disguised as a young man. He came up to me and took my hand, saying, 'My poor unhappy man, where are you going over this mountaintop, alone and without knowing the way? Your men are shut up in Circe's pigsties. You surely do not believe that you can set them free? I can tell you that you will never get back. You will have to stay there with the rest of

---

[5] **wand**—thin rod, twig, or stick often used to perform magic.

them. But never mind, I will protect you. Take this **herb**[6] and keep it with you when you go to Circe's house. It is a charm that will protect you.

"'Let me tell you the wicked witchcraft that Circe will try to practice upon you. She will mix a drink for you, and she will drug the grain with which she makes it. But she will not be able to charm you, because the herb I shall give you will prevent her spells from working. When Circe strikes you with her wand, draw your sword and jump upon her as though you were going to kill her. She will then be frightened and will want you to go to bed with her. You must not refuse her. But you must make her swear that she will plan no further trouble for you. If you do not, she will make you fit for nothing.'

"As he spoke, he pulled the herb out of the ground and showed it to me. The root was black, while the flower was as white as milk. The gods call it Moly. Mortal men cannot dig it up, but the gods can do whatever they like.

"Then Hermes went back to high Olympus, where the gods live. I went on to the house of Circe. When I got to the gates, I called the goddess. She came down, opened the door, and asked me to

---

[6] **herb**—any of various plants that smell good and are often used in medicines.

come in. I followed her—much troubled in my mind. She mixed a drink for me in a golden **goblet**,[7] but she drugged it. When I had drunk it without its charming me, she struck me with her wand. 'There now,' she cried, 'be off to the pigsty, and make your bed with the rest of them!'

"**B**ut I rushed at her with my sword drawn as though I would kill her. She fell with a loud scream, grabbed my knees, and said, 'Who are you? From what place and people have you come? How can it be that my drugs have no power to **bewitch**[8] you? No man has ever been able to stand so much as a taste of the herb I gave you. You must be spell-proof. Surely you must be the bold hero Odysseus, who Hermes always said would come here some day while on his way home from Troy. Put away your sword and let us go to bed.'

"And I answered, 'Circe, how can you expect me to be friendly with you when you have just turned all my men into pigs? You must mean to trick me when you ask me to go to bed with you. You will unman me and make me fit for nothing.

---

[7] **goblet**—drinking cup that has a stem and base.

[8] **bewitch**—place under one's power by magic or spell.

I shall not go with you unless you will first swear to plot no further harm against me.'

"So she swore at once as I had told her. When she had completed her oath, I went with her.

"Meanwhile her four servants set about their work. As soon as one servant had finished washing me and anointing me with oil, she dressed me in a good shirt. Another servant then brought me bread and offered me many good things. Circe told me to eat, but I would not. I ignored what was before me, still moody and suspicious.

" 'Odysseus, why do you sit there refusing both meat and drink? Are you still suspicious? You do not need to be. I have already promised that I will not hurt you.' "

When Circe saw me sitting there without eating, she said, 'Odysseus, why do you sit there refusing both meat and drink? Are you still suspicious? You do not need to be. I have already promised that I will not hurt you.'

"And I said, 'Circe, if you want me to eat and drink, you must free my men and bring them to me that I may see them with my own eyes.'

"When I had said this, she went straight through the court with her wand in her hand and opened the pigsty doors. My men came out like so many hogs and stood looking at her. She anointed each with another magic oil. Their bristles fell off, and they became men again. They were younger and much taller and better-looking than before. They knew me at once, grabbed me by the hand, and wept for joy. Circe was so sorry for them that she said, 'Odysseus, go back at once to the sea where you have left your ship. First draw it onto the land. Then hide all your property in some cave, and come back here with your men.'

"I agreed to this and went back to the seashore. I found the rest of my men there, weeping for the others they thought were forever lost. When they saw me, they surrounded me. 'Sir,' they said, 'we are so glad to see you back. But tell us all about what happened.'

"I said, 'We must draw our ship onto the land. Then come with me as fast as you can to Circe's house. You will find your comrades eating and drinking in the midst of plenty.'

"The men would have come with me at once, but Eurylochus tried to hold them back. He said, 'Alas, what will become of us? Do not rush on to your ruin by going to the house of Circe. She will turn us all into pigs or wolves or lions, bound by her magic, and we shall have to keep guard over her house. Remember how the Cyclops treated us when we went inside his cave. It was all through Odysseus's carelessness that those men lost their lives!'

"When I heard him, I was tempted to draw my sword and cut his head off. But the men said, 'Sir, let this fellow stay here and look after the ship. Take the rest of us with you to Circe's house.'

"So we all went, and Eurylochus was not left behind after all. Later on, he came too, because he feared my scolding.

"Meanwhile Circe had seen that the men left with her were washed and anointed with olive oil. She had also given them woolen cloaks and shirts. When we came, we found them all comfortably at dinner in her house. As soon as the men saw each other face-to-face, they wept for joy. Circe came up to me and said: 'Odysseus, tell your men to stop crying. I know how much you have all suffered at sea, and how cruelly you were treated, but that is over now. So stay here, and eat and drink till you are strong once more. You keep thinking of the hardships you have suffered during your travels. You have no more cheerfulness left in you.'

"We stayed with Circe for a whole year, feasting upon meat and wine. But when the year had passed, my men called me apart and said, 'Sir, it is time you began to think about going home, if you wish to see your house and **native**[9] country at all!'

"Thus did they speak, and I agreed. When the sun went down, I got into bed with Circe and pleaded with her: 'Circe,' said I, 'please keep your promise to help me on my homeward voyage. I want to get back and so do my men.'

"The goddess answered, 'Odysseus, there is another journey that you must take before you can sail homeward. You must go to the house of **Hades**[10] and of dread **Persephone**[11] to speak to the ghost of the blind prophet Teiresias. To him alone has Persephone left his understanding, even in death.'

"I sat up in bed and wept. When I was tired of weeping, I said, 'And who shall guide me upon this voyage? No man has ever sailed to the land of death.'

---

[9] **native**—place of one's birth.
[10] **Hades**—the god (and name) of the underworld.
[11] **Persephone**—goddess abducted by Hades, who then married her.

"'You will need no guide,' she answered. 'Raise your mast, set your white sails, and the north wind will blow you there itself. When your ship has traveled the waters of Oceanus, you will reach the fertile shore of Persephone's country. There beach your ship upon the shore of Oceanus. Go straight to the dark home of Hades.

"'When you have reached this spot, dig a **trench**.[12] Pour into it a drink offering to all the dead. Promise them that when you go back to Ithaca you will sacrifice a **barren**[13] **heifer**[14] to them. Promise that Teiresias shall have a black sheep all to himself, the finest in all your flocks.'

"It was daybreak by the time she was done speaking. I went about among my men and spoke kindly to each of them: 'You must not lie sleeping here any longer,' I said. 'We must be going.'

"When I had the men together, I said to them, 'You think you are about to start home again. But Circe has explained to me that we have to go to the house of Hades and Persephone to speak with the ghost of the prophet Teiresias.'

---

[12] **trench**—deep ditch.

[13] **barren**—not able to produce offspring.

[14] **heifer**—young cow.

"The men were brokenhearted. They threw themselves on the ground, groaning and tearing their hair. When we reached the seashore, Circe brought the ram and the ewe. She passed through the midst of us without our knowing it. For who can see the comings and goings of a god, if the god does not wish to be seen?"

BOOK XI

After Circe had told him that he must consult the blind prophet Teiresias, Odysseus sailed next to the dark underworld of Hades, home of the dead. Here he spoke with the ghost of Teiresias. He foretold Odysseus's future, in which Teiresias saw many fearful things.

"When we had got down to the seashore, we drew our ship into the water. We also put the sheep on board and took our places, weeping with great sadness. Circe, that great and clever goddess, sent us a fair wind that kept our sails well filled. But when the sun went down, we got into the deep waters of the river Oceanus. There lies the city of the Men of Winter, who live in mist and darkness. When we arrived there, we beached the ship, took the sheep out, and went along by the waters of Oceanus till we came to the place Circe told us to find.

"Here I drew my sword and dug a trench. I made a drink offering to all the dead. I promised them that when I got back to Ithaca, I would sacrifice a barren heifer for them. I also promised that Teiresias should have a black sheep to himself, the best in all my flocks. When I had prayed sufficiently to the dead, I cut the throats of the two sheep and let the blood run into the trench. Then the ghosts came trooping up from Erebus.

"There were brides, young bachelors, old men worn out with hard work, maids who had been crossed in love, and brave men who had been killed in battle, with their armor still covered in blood. From every side they came and approached the trench with screams that made me turn pale with fear. I would not let the poor ghosts come near the blood till Teiresias had answered my questions.

"The first ghost that came was that of my comrade Elpenor. We had left his body unmourned and unburied in Circe's house, for we had had too much else to do. I was very sorry for him and cried when I saw him. 'Elpenor,' said I, 'how did you come down here into this gloom and darkness? You got here on foot more quickly than I have with my ship.'

"'Sir,' he sighed, 'it was all bad luck, and my own mistakes. I was lying asleep on the top of Circe's house. I fell right off the roof and broke my neck, so my soul came down to the house of Hades. And now I beg you, do what I shall now ask you. When you leave Hades, you will again head your ship for the Aegean island. Do not go there leaving me unmourned and unburied, or heaven's anger may fall upon you. Burn me with whatever armor I have, and build a **cairn**[1] for me on the seashore. This will tell people in days to come what a poor unlucky fellow I was. Plant over my grave the oar I used to row with when I was still alive.' And I said, 'My poor fellow, I will do all that you have asked of me.'

"Then came the ghost of my dead mother Anticleia. I had left her alive when I set out for Troy and was moved to tears when I saw her. But even so, I would not let her come near the blood until I had asked my questions of Teiresias.

"Then came the ghost of the Theban **prophet**[2] Teiresias, with his golden staff in his hand. He said, 'Odysseus, why have you left the light of day and come down to visit the dead in this sad place?

[1] **cairn**—mound of stones built as a marker, such as for a grave.
[2] **prophet**—one who can see into the future and makes predictions about what will happen.

Stand back from the trench and put away your sword that I may drink of the blood and answer your questions truly.

"'Heaven,' said he, 'will make your return home hard for you. I do not think that you will escape the eye of Poseidon, who still holds a bitter **grudge**[3] against you for having blinded his son, the Cyclops.

"'Still, you may get home if you can control yourself and your crew when your ship reaches the Thrinacian island. There you will find the sheep and cattle belonging to Helios, god of the sun, who sees and hears everything. If you leave these flocks un-harmed, you may yet reach Ithaca. But if you harm them, then both your ship and your men will be destroyed. You may escape, but you will return in bad shape after losing all your men, in another man's ship. Your house will be overrun by people who eat your **livestock**[4] and court your wife.

> "'Heaven,' said he, 'will make your return home hard for you. I do not think that you will escape the eye of Poseidon, who still holds a bitter grudge against you for having blinded his son, the Cyclops.'"

---

[3] **grudge**—feeling of anger or dislike because of a real or an imaginary wrong.
[4] **livestock**—animals such as cattle or horses.

"'When you get home, you will take your revenge on these suitors. After you have killed them, you must take an oar and carry it on and on, until you come to a country where the people have never heard of the sea, nor do they know anything about ships and oars. How will you know you're in the right place? A traveler will meet you. He will say it must be a "**winnowing fan**"[5] that you have upon your shoulder. When you hear this, you must stick the oar in the ground and sacrifice a ram, a bull, and a boar to the god Poseidon. Then go home and offer sacrifices to all the gods in heaven, one after the other. As for yourself, death shall come to you from the sea. Your life shall ebb away very gently when you are full of years and peace of mind. Your people shall bless you. All that I have said will come true.'

> "' As for yourself, death shall come to you from the sea. Your life shall ebb away very gently when you are full of years and peace of mind.'"

"'This,' I answered, 'must be as it may please heaven. But tell me true, I see my poor mother's ghost close by us. She is sitting without saying a word. Though I am her own son, she does not

---

[5] **winnowing fan**—fan held to separate wheat from chaff (that is, the good from the bad part of wheat).

remember me. Tell me, sir, how I can make her know me!'

"'That I can soon do,' said he. 'Any ghost you let enter where the blood is will talk with you like a normal person. But if you do not let them have any blood, they will go away again and fade.'

"On this the ghost of Teiresias went back to the halls of Death. I sat still where I was until my mother came up and tasted of the blood. Then she knew me at once. She spoke fondly to me, saying, 'My son, how did you come down to this house of darkness while you are still alive? Are you still trying to find your way home from Troy? Have you never gotten back to Ithaca, nor seen your wife in your own house?'

"'Mother,' said I, 'I came here to speak with the ghost of the Theban prophet Teiresias. I have never yet been near the Achaean land nor set foot on my native country. I have had nothing but misfortunes from the very first day that I set out to fight the Trojans. But tell me, in what way did you die? Did you have a long illness, or did heaven grant you a gentle, easy passage to eternity? Tell me also about my father, and the son whom I left behind me. Tell me also about my wife. Does she live with my son and guard my house? Or has she made the best match she could and married again?'

"My noble mother answered: 'Your wife remains in your house, but she is troubled. She spends her whole time in tears both day and night. But no man takes your place. Telemachus still holds your lands, and your father remains at his old place in the country. He suffers more and more as he grows older. My own end happened this way: heaven did not take me swiftly and painlessly in my own house. My loneliness for you, Odysseus, was the death of me!'

"Thus did we talk, and soon Persephone sent up the ghosts of the wives and daughters of all the most famous men. They gathered in crowds about the blood. I decided that it would be best to draw my sword and keep them from all drinking the blood at once. So they came up one after the other, and each one told me a name and his or her **lineage**.[6]

"It would take me all night if I were to name every one of the heroes' wives and daughters whom I saw. It is time for me to go to bed."

---

[6] **lineage**—forefathers, family history.

Here Odysseus ended, and Alcinous's guests sat spellbound and speechless. Then Arete said to them:

"What do you think of this man, O Phaeacians? Is he not tall and good looking, and is he not clever? Do not be in a hurry to send him away, nor stingy in the presents you make to one who is in such great need."

"This thing shall be done," exclaimed Alcinous, "as surely as I still live and reign over the Phaeacians. Our guest is indeed very anxious to get home. Still we must persuade him to remain with us until tomorrow. By then I shall be able to get together all that I mean to give him. As regards his **escort**,[7] it will be a matter for you all, and for me above others as the chief among you.

And Odysseus answered: "King Alcinous, if you were to ask me to stay here for a whole twelve months, and then speed me on my way, loaded with your noble gifts, I should obey you gladly."

"Odysseus," replied Alcinous, "you tell me whether you saw any of the mighty heroes who went to Troy at the same time as yourself and died there. It is not yet bedtime. Go on, therefore, with

---

[7] **escort**—guide, protector.

your story, for I could stay here listening until tomorrow morning."

"Alcinous," answered Odysseus, "since you so desire, I will tell you the still sadder tale of those of my comrades who did not fall fighting with the Trojans, but died on their return, through the treachery of a wicked woman.

"When Persephone had dismissed the female ghosts, the sad ghost of **Agamemnon**[8] came up to me, surrounded by those who had died with him in the house of Aegisthus. As soon as he had tasted the blood, he knew me. Weeping bitterly, he stretched out his arms toward me to hold me. 'How did you come about your death, King Agamemnon? Did Poseidon raise his winds and waves against you when you were at sea? Or did your enemies make an end of you?'

"'Odysseus,' he answered, 'I was not lost at sea in any storm of Poseidon's raising, nor did my enemies kill me. Aegisthus and my wicked wife were the death of me. Aegisthus asked me to his house, feasted me, and then killed me as though I were a beast in a slaughterhouse. All around me, my comrades were slain like sheep or

---

[8] **Agamemnon**—a king who led the Greeks against the Trojans in the Trojan War.

pigs for a great banquet. You never saw anything so truly sad as the way in which we fell. I heard Priam's daughter Cassandra scream as my wife Clytemnestra killed her close beside me. I lay dying upon the earth with the sword in my body and raised my hands to kill my wicked wife, but she slipped away. She would not even close my lips or eyes when I was dying. There is nothing in this world so cruel and so shameless as a woman who murders her own husband. Her crime has brought disgrace on herself and all women who shall come after.

> "'Be sure, therefore,' continued Agamemnon, 'not to be too friendly even with your own wife. Do not tell her all that you know perfectly well yourself. Tell her a part only, and keep quiet about the rest.'"

"'Be sure, therefore,' continued Agamemnon, 'not to be too friendly even with your own wife. Do not tell her all that you know perfectly well yourself. Tell her a part only, and keep quiet about the rest. One thing I will advise. Land your ship in secret on the island. Give no warning—the day of faithful wives is gone forever.'

"The ghosts of other dead men stood near me, and each told me his own sad tale. I would have seen still others of them, but so many thousands of ghosts came round me and cried so that I was frightened. I hurried back to my ship and ordered my men to go on board at once. They boarded the ship and took their places and then went down the stream of the river Oceanus."

BOOK XII

*From the house of Hades, Odysseus returned to Circe,
who warned him of the dangers ahead. They sailed
by the rocks of the Sirens and Scylla and Charybdis.
Landing on the island of Sicily, Odysseus's men killed
the fine cattle there, the property of the sun god.
In punishment, Zeus destroyed their ship with his
thunderbolts. Odysseus alone escaped drowning and
was stranded on Calypso's isle. With this he brings his
tale to an end.*

"After we had moved out into the open
sea, we went on till we reached the Aegean
island. When dawn appeared, I sent some men
to Circe's house to fetch the body of my man
Elpenor. After we had wept over him, we per-
formed his funeral rites.

"While we were doing all this, Circe came to us with handmaids bearing bread, roast meats, and ruby-colored wine. She said, 'You have done a bold thing in going alive to the house of Hades. Stay here for the rest of the day, feast your fill, and go on with your voyage at daybreak tomorrow. In the meantime, I will tell Odysseus about your course, so as to prevent more suffering.'

"Then Circe took me away from the others and asked me all about our adventures.

"'If anyone comes too close and hears the singing of the Sirens, his wife and children will never welcome him home again.'"

"'So far, so good,' said she, when I had ended my story. 'Now pay attention to what I am about to tell you. First you will come to the Sirens, who enchant all who come near them. If anyone comes too close and hears the singing of the Sirens, his wife and children will never welcome him home again. The Sirens will sit any man they enchant in a green field and sing his mind away with the sweetness of their songs. So pass by these Sirens. Stop your men's ears with wax that none of them may hear. If you wish to listen, you may get the men to tie you to the mast. If you beg and pray the men to untie you, then they must twist more line around you.

"'When your crew has taken you past these Sirens, you will have two choices before you. On the one hand there are some overhanging rocks against which the deep blue waves beat with terrific fury. The blessed gods call these rocks the Wanderers. Only one ship has ever made it past them. The waves nearby are filled with wreckage and with the bodies of dead men.

"'A second course lies between two rocks. Of these two rocks, one reaches heaven and its peak is lost in a dark cloud. The top is never clear, not even in the summer and early autumn. In the middle of it there is a large cave. Inside it Scylla sits and **yelps**[1] with a voice that sounds like that of a young hound. But she is a dreadful monster. She has twelve feet and six necks of the most amazing length. At the end of each neck she has a frightful head with three rows of teeth that would crunch anyone to death in a moment. No ship has yet gotten past her without losing some men, for she

---

[1] **yelps**—barks or cries in short, sharp bursts, like a dog.

shoots out all her heads at once and carries off a man in each mouth.

"'You will find the other rock lies lower, but they are very close together. A large fir tree in full leaf grows upon it. Under it lies the sucking **whirlpool**[2] of Charybdis. Three times in the day does she spit forth her waters. Three times she sucks them down again. See that you are not there when she is sucking. If you are, Poseidon himself could not save you. You must hug the Scylla side and drive your ship by as fast as you can.

"'Even though you may yourself escape, you will return late, in bad shape, after losing all your men.'"

"'You will now come to the Thrinacian island. Here you will see many herds of cattle and flocks of sheep belonging to the sun god Helios. If you leave these flocks unharmed, you may still reach Ithaca. But if you harm them, then your ship and your comrades will be destroyed. Even though you may yourself escape, you will return late, in bad shape, after losing all your men.'

"Here Circe ended. As dawn appeared, I went on board and told my men to cast off.

---

[2] **whirlpool**—a current of water going around rapidly and violently.

"Then I said to my men, 'My friends, it is not right that one of us alone should know the prophecies that Circe has made me. I will tell you about them, so that whether we live or die, we may do so with our eyes open.'

"I had hardly finished telling everything to the men before we reached the island of the Sirens. Then all of a sudden dead calm came on. So the men rolled up the sails and began rowing. Meanwhile I took a large wheel of wax and cut it up into small pieces with my sword. I worked the wax till it became soft. Then I stopped the ears of all my men. They bound my hands and feet to the mast, but went on rowing themselves. When we were close to the land, the Sirens began their singing.

"'Come here,' they sang, 'great Odysseus, and listen to our voices. No one ever sailed past us without staying to hear the sweetness of our song. He who listens will go on his way not only charmed, but wiser.'

"They sang these words most musically. I longed to hear them further, so I made signs to my men that they should set me free. But they bound me with still stronger bonds till we had gotten out of hearing of the Sirens' voices. Then my men took the wax from their ears and untied me.

"Immediately after we had moved past the island, I saw a great wave, and I heard a loud roaring sound. The men were so frightened that they let go of their oars.

"'My friends,' said I, 'this is not the first time that we have been in danger. Now let us all do as I say. Trust in Zeus and row with all your strength. Turn the ship away from these steaming rapids and hug the rock, or you will be the death of us.'

"So they did as I told them. But I said nothing about the awful monster Scylla, for I knew the men could do nothing about it.

"Then, frightened, we entered the straits. The dread Charybdis kept sucking up the water. As she spit it up, it was like the water in a pot when it is boiling over upon a great fire. The spray reached the top of the rocks on either side. When Charybdis began to suck again, we could see the water all inside whirling round and round. It made a deafening sound as it broke against the rocks. The men were at their wits' ends for fear.

"Then Scylla pounced down suddenly upon us and snatched up my six best men. In a moment I saw their hands and feet high above me, struggling in the air as Scylla carried them off. I heard them call out my name in one last sorrowful cry. Scylla threw them on her rock and munched them up. They screamed and stretched out their hands to me in their agony. This was the worst sight that I saw throughout all my voyages.

> **"I heard them call out my name in one last sorrowful cry. Scylla threw them on her rock and munched them up."**

"When we had passed the Wandering rocks, we reached an island, where there were cattle and sheep belonging to the sun god Helios. I remembered what the blind prophet Teiresias had told me, and how carefully Circe had warned me to stay clear of the island of the blessed sun god. So I said to the men, 'I know you are exhausted, but the prophet Teiresias and Circe warned me that our worst danger would lie on this island. Head the ship, therefore, away from the island.'

"The men were in despair at this. Eurylochus at once gave me a rude answer. 'Odysseus,' said he, 'you are cruel. You are very strong yourself and never get worn out. Even though your men are tired and want to sleep, you will not let them land and cook themselves a good supper upon this island.'

"Thus spoke Eurylochus, and the men approved his words. I saw that heaven meant us mischief and said, 'You force me to yield, for you are many against one. But each of you must swear that you will not kill any cattle or sheep.'

"Then a hurricane blew up, and we were unable to set sail the next day. 'My friends,' said I, 'we have meat and drink in the ship, so let us not touch the cattle, or we shall suffer for it. These cattle and sheep belong to the mighty sun, who sees and hears everything.' Again they promised they would obey.

"For a whole month the wind blew steadily from the south. As long as corn and wine held out, the men did not touch the cattle. But when they had eaten all there was in the ship, they were forced to fish and catch birds, for they were starving.

> "'My friends,' said I, 'we have meat and drink in the ship, so let us not touch the cattle, or we shall suffer for it. These cattle and sheep belong to the mighty sun, who sees and hears everything.'"

One day I went to pray to heaven to show me some means of getting away. When I had found a place sheltered from the wind, I prayed to all the gods on Olympus. By and by, they sent me off into a sweet sleep.

"Meanwhile Eurylochus had been giving evil advice to the men. 'Listen to me,' said he, 'all deaths are bad enough, but there is none so bad as **famine**.[3] Why should we not choose the best of these cows and offer them in sacrifice to the immortal gods? If we ever get back to Ithaca, we can build a fine temple to the sun god and decorate it with every kind of ornament. But if he wants to destroy our ship out of revenge, I for one would rather drown and be done with it than be starved to death.'

"Thus spoke Eurylochus, and once again the men approved his words. Now the cattle were grazing not far from the ship. The men drove in the best of them, and they all stood round the cattle saying their prayers. When the men were done praying, they killed the cows and **dressed**[4] their **carcasses**.[5]

---

[3] **famine**—severe hunger, starvation.

[4] **dressed**—cleaned in preparation for cooking.

[5] **carcasses**—dead bodies of animals, especially ones killed for food.

"By this time I awoke and went back to the ship. As I drew near, I began to smell hot roasted meat. I groaned out a prayer to the immortal gods. 'Father Zeus,' I exclaimed, 'and all you other gods, you have done me a cruel trick by putting me to sleep. See what these men have done while I was away.'

"Meanwhile the sun god learned we had been killing his cows. He flew into a great rage and said to the immortals, 'Father Zeus, and all you other gods, I must have revenge on the crew of Odysseus's ship. They have killed my cows.'

"'Sun,' said Zeus, 'go on shining upon us gods and upon mankind over the fruitful earth. I will break their ship into little pieces with a bolt of white lightning as soon as they get out to sea.'

"As soon as I got down to the seashore, I scolded each one of my men.

"But for six days my men kept driving in the best cows and feasting upon them. On the seventh day, the winds grew calm. We therefore went on board the ship and sailed to sea. As soon as we were all well away from the island, a black cloud appeared over our ship, and the sea grew dark beneath it. In another moment we were caught by a terrific storm.

"Then Zeus let fly his thunderbolts. The ship went round and round, and it was filled with fire as the lightning struck it. The men all fell into the sea. They bobbed awhile in the waves, but Zeus had drowned them.

"I stuck to the ship until it broke into pieces. I was carried along for nine days. On the tenth night, the gods left me on the Ogygian island, where the great and powerful goddess Calypso lives. She took me in and was kind to me, but I need say no more about this, for I told you about that yesterday."

BOOK XIII

Odysseus is given more rich gifts by Alcinous and his people. Then he is sent away at night in a ship to Ithaca. On arrival he is carried, sleeping, ashore and set gently down with his treasure. When Odysseus wakes, Athena appears and tells him he is in Ithaca. She then changes him into an ugly old beggar.

Thus did Odysseus speak, and they were enthralled by his story. The Phaecian King Alcinous and his people presented Odysseus with more gifts.

The next day, Alcinous held a farewell dinner for Odysseus. Afterward, Odysseus thanked Alcinous and the Phaeacians:

"Sir, and all of you, farewell. You have fulfilled my heart's desire and given me presents. May heaven grant you every good grace. May no evil thing come among your people."

Odysseus then left them and got on the ship they had for him. They had spread out a rug so that he might sleep soundly in the back of the ship. Odysseus lay down without a word. The crew took their places and began rowing out to sea. Odysseus fell into a deep, sweet, and almost deathlike sleep.

After sailing for days, they landed, lifted Odysseus with his rug out of the ship, and lay him down upon the sand still fast asleep. Then they took out the gifts that the Phaeacians had given him. They put these all together, so no one could steal them before Odysseus awoke. Then they made their way home again.

At long last Odysseus woke once more upon his own soil. He had been away so long that he did not recognize it. Moreover, Zeus's daughter Athena had made it a foggy day. She wished to tell him everything without anyone recognizing him until he had taken his revenge upon the wicked suitors.

Then Athena came up to him disguised as a young shepherd. Odysseus was glad when he saw her.

"My friend," said he, "you are the first person I have met in this country. I beg you to be kind to me. Tell me, what land and country is this?"

Athena answered, "Stranger, you must be very **ignorant**,[1] or must have come from somewhere a long way off, not to know what country this is. The name of the country is Ithaca."

Odysseus was glad at finding himself in his own country, but he did not fully believe it yet. He pretended he was from Crete and had never been in Ithaca before. He then made up a story explaining how he landed there.

> "Stranger, you must be very ignorant, or must have come from somewhere a long way off, not to know what country this is. The name of the country is Ithaca."

Athena smiled. She then took the form of a woman, fair, stately, and wise. "You are too clever," she said. "No more of this, though! We are alike. You are the best storyteller, and I am famous for wisdom—and deceptions—among the gods. Did you guess that I am Athena, daughter of Zeus?"

Odysseus answered, "In good truth, goddess, advise me how I shall best get revenge. Stand by my side and put your courage into my heart. I will fight three hundred men, if you, goddess, will be with me."

---

[1] **ignorant**—unaware of one's surroundings.

"Trust me for that," said she, "I will begin by disguising you so that no one shall know you. I will cover your body with wrinkles. I will clothe you in rags. Then go at once to the **swineherd**[2] who is in charge of your pigs. Stay with him and find out how things are going, while I go to see your son, who is with King Menelaus at Sparta."

As she spoke, Athena touched him with her wand and covered him with wrinkles. She changed his clothes and threw an old rag of a wrap about him.

After they had made their plans, they parted. Athena went straight to Sparta to get Telemachus.

---

[2] **swineherd**—person who tends or looks after swine (pigs).

BOOK XIV

*Odysseus finds the hut of his swineherd Eumaeus. He
is made welcome and learns the news of home. He does
not reveal himself to Eumaeus.*

Odysseus walked until he reached the place
where Athena had said that he would find the
swineherd. He found Eumaeus sitting in front
of his hut. There were fifty pigs. The boars slept
outside and were much fewer in number, for
the suitors kept on eating them. The herdsman's
four hounds, which were as fierce as wolves,
guarded them.

When the hounds saw Odysseus, they began
barking furiously and flew at him.

He would have been torn apart if the swineherd had not driven the dogs off. Then he said to Odysseus: "Old man, the dogs were likely to have torn you apart, and then you would have gotten me into trouble. The gods have given me quite enough worries about that, for I have lost the best of masters. I have to attend swine for other people to eat, while my master, if he still lives, is starving in some distant land. But come inside. Tell me where you come from, and all about yourself."

As he spoke, he went to where the young sucking pigs were penned. He picked out two, which he brought back with him and sacrificed. He cooked the meat and set it before Odysseus.

Odysseus began eating and drinking greedily without a word, planning his revenge. When he had eaten enough, he said to Eumaeus, "My friend, who was this master of yours? Tell me who he was, in case I may have met with such a person. I may be able to give you news of him, for I have traveled much."

Eumaeus answered: "Old man, no traveler who comes here with news will get Odysseus's wife and son to believe his story. Everyone who finds his way to Ithaca goes to my mistress and tells her lies. She takes them in, makes much of them, and asks them all kinds of questions, crying all the time for her lost husband. But the wolves and birds of prey have long since torn Odysseus to pieces, or the fishes of the sea have eaten him. His bones are lying buried deep in sand upon some shore. He is dead and done, and a bad business it is for all his friends—for me especially. Go where I may, I shall never find so good a master. He was very fond of me, and took such care of me that wherever he may be I shall always honor his memory."

> "Odysseus will return very soon to get revenge on all those who are mistreating his wife and son."

"My friend," replied Odysseus, "you seem so sure that your master will never come home again. But I will swear that he is coming. Odysseus will return very soon to get revenge on all those who are mistreating his wife and son."

To this Eumaeus answered: "Old man, let us talk about something else. Do not keep on reminding me of all this. It always pains me when anyone speaks about my honored master. And now, tell me who you are and where you come from. Tell me what kind of ship you came in and how your crew brought you to Ithaca, for you cannot have come by land."

Odysseus then invented a long story about being the son of a slave and having married into a rich family. He claimed to have heard news of Odysseus's return.

When Odysseus had finished his story, Eumaeus said: "Poor unhappy stranger, I have found the story of your misfortunes extremely interesting. But the part about Odysseus is not right. You will never get me to believe it. I know about the return of my master. The gods, one and all of them, hate Odysseus, or they would have taken him before. Now the storm winds have blown him away, we know not where. Do not try to give me false hopes."

Odysseus answered: "I see that you are of an unbelieving mind. I have given you my promise, and yet you do not believe me. Let us then make a bargain. If your master comes home, give me a cloak and shirt of good wear, and send me to Dulichium—it is a pleasant island. But if he does not come as I say he will, set your men on me. Tell them to throw me from a high cliff as a warning not to go around the country telling lies."

BOOK XV

Meanwhile Athena appears to Telemachus at Menelaus's house and tells him to return home. Odysseus stays on with the swineherd Eumaeus, who tells him the story of his life. Telemachus lands and comes straight to the swineherd's hut.

Athena went to Sparta to tell Odysseus's son Telemachus to return at once. She found him and King Nestor's son Pisistratus sleeping in Menelaus's house. Pisistratus was fast asleep, but Telemachus got no rest all night for thinking of his unhappy father. Athena went close to him and said:

"Telemachus, you should not remain so far away from home any longer. You should not leave your property with such dangerous people in your house. They will eat up everything you have. Ask Menelaus to send you home at once.

"Let me tell you also of another matter. The chief men among the suitors are lying in wait for you in the ocean between Ithaca and Same. They mean to kill you before you can reach home. Sail night and day, and keep your ship well away from the islands. A god who cares for you will make a fair wind blow. As soon as you get to Ithaca, send your ship and men on to the town. But you go straight to the swineherd who has charge of your pigs. Stay with him for the night. Then send him to your mother to tell her that you have gotten back safe from Pylos."

Then Athena went back to Olympus.

Day began to break. Menelaus, who had already risen, came toward them. When Telemachus saw him, he threw a cloak over his shoulders and went out to meet him. "Menelaus," said he, "send me back now to my own country, for I want to get home."

Menelaus answered: "Telemachus, if you want to go, I will not stop you." Telemachus and Pisistratus then left almost immediately.

At Pylos, after they arrived at the ship, Pisistratus said farewell to Telemachus, who called the men together and gave his orders. "Now, my men," said he, "get everything in order on board the ship. Let us set out at once."

Meanwhile Odysseus and the swineherd were eating their meal in the hut. As soon as they had had enough to eat and drink, Odysseus began trying to test the swineherd. He wanted to see whether Eumaeus would continue to treat him kindly and ask him to stay or would send him off to the city. He said:

"Eumaeus, tomorrow I want to go away and begin begging about the town. I wish to be no more trouble to you or to your men. Please show me the way. I should also like to go to the house of Odysseus and bring news of her husband to Queen Penelope. I could then go about among the suitors to see if they will give me a dinner. I should soon make them an excellent servant in all sorts of ways. I would put fresh wood on the fire, chop fuel, carve, cook, pour out wine, and do all those services that poor men have to do for their betters."

The swineherd was very much disturbed when he heard this. "Heaven help me," he exclaimed, "whatever can have put such an idea into your head? Stay where you are. You are not in anybody's way. I do not mind your being here, nor do any of the others. When Telemachus comes home, he will give you a shirt and cloak and will send you wherever you want to go."

Odysseus answered, "I hope you may be as dear to the gods as you are to me. You have saved me from pain and homelessness. Since you press me to stay here, tell me about Odysseus's mother and father. Are they still living, or are they already dead and in the house of Hades?"

> Odysseus answered, "I hope you may be as dear to the gods as you are to me. You have saved me from pain and homelessness."

"Laertes is still living," replied Eumaeus, "and prays to heaven to let him depart peacefully in his own house. He is terribly upset about his son, and also about the death of his wife. She came to an unhappy end through sorrow for her son."

Far into the night, Odysseus and Eumaeus talked. In the meantime, Telemachus and his crew were nearing land. As they did, Telemachus said, "Take the ship on to the town, but leave me here. I want to look after the herdsmen Eumaeus on one of my farms. In the evening, when I have seen all I want, I will come down to the city."

As the ship sailed away toward the city, Telemachus ran as fast as he could. Soon he reached the **homestead**[1] of the excellent swineherd, who was so devoted a servant to his master.

---

[1] **homestead**—a home and the land on which it is located.

BOOK XVI

Telemachus sends Eumaeus into the town to tell Penelope that her son is safely back. Athena then changes Odysseus back to his own likeness. He reveals himself to Telemachus and tells his son of his plan for killing the suitors.

Odysseus and the swineherd Eumaeus were in the hut getting breakfast ready, for they had sent the men out with the pigs. Odysseus heard the sound of footsteps approaching and noticed that the dogs did not bark. He said to Eumaeus:

"Eumaeus, I hear footsteps. I suppose one of your men or someone you know is coming here, for the dogs are not barking."

The words were hardly out of his mouth before Odysseus's tall son stood at the door. Eumaeus jumped to his feet. The bowls in which he was mixing wine fell from his hands as he ran toward his master.

"So you have come home, Telemachus," said Eumaeus, "When I heard you had gone to Pylos, I was sure I was never going to see you any more. Come in, my dear child, and sit down. It is not very often you come into the country to see us herdsmen."

Answered Telemachus, "I have come now because I want to see you. I also want to learn whether my mother is still at her old home or whether someone else has married her."

"She is still at the house," replied Eumaeus. "She has done nothing but weep, both night and day."

Telemachus crossed the stone threshold and came inside. Odysseus (still disguised as an old man) rose from his seat, but Telemachus stopped him. "Sit down, stranger," said he. "I can easily find another seat."

Telemachus said to Eumaeus, "Old friend, where does this stranger come from? How did he get to Ithaca?"

To this Eumaeus answered: "My son, I will tell you the truth. He says he is from Crete. At this moment he is running away from a ship. He has come to stay at my hut. Do whatever you like with him, only remember that he has humbly asked for your help."

"I am very sad," said Telemachus. "Still, I will find him a cloak and shirt, a sword and sandals. I will send him wherever he wants to go. Or if you like, you can keep him here at your hut. I will send him clothes and food that he may be no burden on you. But I will not have him go to my mother's house and be near the suitors. They will surely treat him badly."

Then Odysseus said, "Sir, I am shocked by what you have said about the suitors' behavior. If I were son to Odysseus, I would rather die fighting in my own house than see such disgraceful behavior."

> *"I will tell you truly everything. There is no bad feeling between me and my people. But my house has been taken over. The chiefs from all the neighboring islands and all the principal men of Ithaca are eating up my house as they court my mother."*

And Telemachus answered: "I will tell you truly everything. There is no bad feeling between me and my people. But my house has been taken over. The chiefs from all the neighboring islands, and all the principal men of Ithaca are eating up my house as they court my mother.

She neither says point-blank that she will not marry, nor does she bring matters to an end.

"Eumaeus, old friend, go at once and tell Penelope that I have safely returned from Pylos. Do not tell anyone else, for there are many who are plotting against me."

"I understand you," replied Eumaeus. "Should I let poor Laertes know that you are returned? They tell me that, from the day on which you left for Pylos, he has neither eaten nor drunk as he ought to do. Nor does he look after his farm. He sits weeping."

"I am sorry for him," answered Telemachus, "but we must leave him to himself just now. Go and give your message to Penelope. Then hurry back again."

Eumaeus then started for the town. Athena then came up to the hut in the form of a woman. She revealed herself to Odysseus, but Telemachus could not see her. Athena motioned to Odysseus, so he left the hut and stood before her. Then she said to him, "Odysseus, it is now time for you to tell your son who you are. Do not keep him in the dark any longer. Make your plans for the killing of the suitors, and then head for the town. I will soon join you."

As she spoke she touched him with her golden wand, and he looked like himself once again. Then she went away, and Odysseus came back inside the hut. His son was astonished when he saw him. He turned his eyes away for fear he might be looking upon a god.

Odysseus said, "I am no god. I am your father."

"Stranger," said he, "how suddenly you have changed from what you were a moment or two ago. You are dressed differently and your color is not the same. Are you one of the gods who live in heaven?"

Odysseus said, "I am no god. I am your father." As he spoke, he kissed his son, and a tear fell from his cheek.

Then Telemachus began to weep. He asked, "In what ship, my dear father, did your crew bring you to Ithaca? From what nation did they come?"

"I will tell you the truth, my son," replied Odysseus. "It was the Phaeacians who brought me here. They are great sailors. They took me over the sea while I was fast asleep. Then they landed me in Ithaca, after giving me many presents. These gifts are lying in a cave. I have come here on the suggestion of Athena so we may plan out how to kill our enemies. First, give me the names of the suitors. I must learn who, and how many, they are. I can then decide whether we two can fight them ourselves, or whether we must find others to help us."

To this Telemachus answered: "Father, the task you talk of is a very great one. There are fifty-two youths from Dulichium, and they have six servants. From Same there are twenty-four. Twenty young Achaeans are from Zacynthus, and twelve are from Ithaca itself."

Odysseus replied, "Do you think Athena and her father Zeus would be sufficient? Or should I try to find someone else as well?"

"Athena and Zeus are a couple of good allies," answered Telemachus. "Though they live high up among the clouds, they have power over both gods and men."

"Now," continued Odysseus, "return home early tomorrow morning and act as usual. Later on the swineherd will bring me to the city looking like a miserable old beggar. If you see them mistreating me, do nothing.

"When Athena gives me a signal, I will nod my head to you. At this, you must collect all of the armor that is in the house and hide it in the storeroom. Make some excuse when the suitors ask you why you are removing it. Leave a sword and a spear for yourself and me so that we can snatch them up at any moment. Zeus and Athena will then soon quiet these people with their magic. There is also another matter. Let no one know that Odysseus is within the house, not Laertes, nor the swineherd here, and not even Penelope. You and I will test the women and the servants to see who is on our side and who is against us."

While they talked, the ship that had brought Telemachus and his crew from Pylos reached the town of Ithaca. When they drew the ship on to the land, they sent a servant to tell Penelope. The swineherd Eumaeus reached the king's hall at the same time. Eumaeus drew close to Penelope and said all that her son had asked him to tell her.

The suitors were surprised and angry at what had happened. They held a meeting near the main entrance. Eurymachus, son of Polybus, was the first to speak.

"My friends," said he, "this voyage of Telemachus's is a very serious matter."

"Good heavens," said Antinous, "see how the gods have saved this man from destruction! Let us capture and kill him. Then we can divide his property among us. We can let his mother and the man who marries her have the house."

Then Amphinomus, Penelope's favorite of the suitors, rose to speak. "My friends," said he, "I am not in favor of killing Telemachus. Let us first ask the advice of the gods."

Penelope then decided to show herself to the suitors. She knew of the plot against Telemachus. She went down to the court with her maidens. When she reached the suitors, she scolded Antinous, saying:

"Madman, why should you try to kill Telemachus? Do you not remember how Odysseus rescued your father from his enemies? Now you ruin his property without paying for it, you try to marry his wife, and you try to kill his son. Leave off doing so, and stop the others also."

To this Eurymachus lied: "Take heart, Queen Penelope, and do not trouble yourself about these matters. I will kill any man who tries to lay hands upon your son Telemachus. He has nothing to fear from the hands of us suitors."

Then Penelope went upstairs again. In the evening Eumaeus returned to Odysseus and his son, who were just preparing supper. Athena came to Odysseus and turned him into an old man with a stroke of her wand. She dressed him in his old clothes again so that the swineherd would not recognize him as Odysseus.

Telemachus was the first to speak. "So you have returned," said he. "What is the news of the town? Have the suitors returned, or are they still waiting to kill me on my way home?"

"I did not think of asking about that," replied Eumaeus, "but I saw a ship coming into harbor with a number of men in her. They had many shields and spears. I thought it was the suitors, but I cannot be sure."

On hearing this, Telemachus smiled to his father, but did not let Eumaeus see him.

Then they ate their meal and lay down to sleep.

BOOK XVII

Telemachus is welcomed home by his mother Penelope. He tells her what he heard from Menelaus about Odysseus. Odysseus, again disguised as an old beggar, sets out with Eumaeus for the town. Telemachus gives Odysseus food, but a suitor, Antinous, insults him and hits him.

When dawn appeared, Telemachus said to the swineherd, "Old friend, I will now go to the town and show myself to my mother. As for this poor stranger, take him to the town and let him beg there. I have trouble enough of my own. I cannot be **burdened**[1] with other people."

Then Odysseus said: "Sir, I do not want to stay here. A beggar can always do better in town than in

---

[1] **burdened**—responsible for.

the country. Let this man take me to the town as soon as I am warmed by the fire."

Telemachus went off through the yards, planning his revenge upon the suitors. When he reached home, he went inside.

Nurse Euryclea saw him before anyone else did. She burst out crying as she ran up to him. All the other maids came up too and covered his head and shoulders with their kisses. Penelope came out of her room and wept as she threw her arms about her son. "Light of my eyes," she cried, as she spoke fondly to him, "so you are come home again! I was afraid I was never going to see you any more. But come, tell me what you saw."

"I have had a narrow escape," answered Telemachus. "Now if the gods will only grant us our revenge upon the suitors. I must now go to bring home a stranger who has come back with me from Pylos. I sent him on with my crew and told my good friend Piraeus to look after him till I could come for him myself."

"Telemachus," Penelope said, "I shall go upstairs and lie down on that sad couch, which I have watered with my tears from the day Odysseus set out for Troy. You failed, however, to tell me, whether or not you had heard anything about the return of your father."

"I will tell you the truth," replied her son. "We went to Pylos and saw King Nestor. He took me to his house and treated me very well. But he had not heard a word from anyone about Odysseus. So he sent me with a horse to Menelaus. Menelaus told me he could see Odysseus on an island resting sadly in the house of the nymph Calypso. She was keeping him prisoner, and he could not reach his home, for he had no ships or sailors to take him over the sea. The gods then gave me a fair wind and soon brought me safe home again."

With these words Telemachus moved the heart of Penelope.

Presently Odysseus and the swineherd Eumaeus came to the house. Odysseus said:

"Eumaeus, this house of Odysseus is a very fine place. No matter how far you go, you will find few like it. I think that there are many people feasting within it, for I smell roasted meat. I hear a sound of music, which the gods have made to go along with feasting."

Then Eumaeus said: "Let us think what will be our best plan. Will you go inside first and join the suitors? Or will you wait here and let me go in first?"

And Odysseus answered: "Go in first and leave me here where I am. I am quite used to being beaten and having things thrown at me."

Telemachus saw Eumaeus and asked him to come and sit beside him. So he sat down at Telemachus's table, and the servant brought him food and drink.

Odysseus then came inside, looking like a poor miserable old beggar, leaning on his staff, his clothes in rags. He sat down at the door. Telemachus took a whole loaf from the bread basket, with as much meat as he could hold in his two hands. He said to Eumaeus, "Take this to the stranger, and tell him to go around and beg from the suitors. A beggar must not be shamefaced."

So Eumaeus went up to him and said, "Stranger, Telemachus sends you this and says you are to go the round of the suitors begging."

Odysseus answered, "May King Zeus grant all happiness to Telemachus and fulfill the desire of his heart."

Then with both hands he took what Telemachus had sent him and ate it. Athena then told Odysseus, "Beg pieces of bread from each one of the suitors. You will then be able to see what kind of people they are and to tell the good from the bad."

Odysseus, therefore, went around and put out his hands as though he were a real beggar. Some of them pitied him and were curious about him. They asked one another who he was and from where he came.

Antinous began to abuse the swineherd Eumaeus. "You idiot," he cried. "Why have you brought this man to town? We have enough tramps and beggars already to pester us."

And Eumaeus answered: "Antinous, your words are evil. You are always harder on Odysseus's servants than any of the other suitors are, and on me above all. But I do not care so long as Telemachus and Penelope are alive and here."

Telemachus said, "Hush, do not answer him. Antinous has the bitterest tongue of all the suitors."

As Antinous spoke, he picked up a **stool**[2] from under the table and acted as though he would throw it at Odysseus. But the other suitors all gave him something and filled his bag with bread and meat. He was about to go back to eat what the

---

[2] **stool**—a backless and armless seat supported on legs.

suitors had given him, but he first went to Antinous and said:

"Sir, give me something. You are not the poorest man here. You seem to be a chief among them all, and therefore you should be the better giver. I too was a rich man once and had a fine house of my own. In those days I gave to many a tramp, no matter who he might be or what he wanted."

Then Antinous said: "What god sent such a pest to bother us during our dinner? Get out."

Then Antinous said: "What god sent such a pest to bother us during our dinner? Get out."

With these words, Antinous threw a stool at him and hit him on the right shoulder blade near the top of his back. Odysseus stood firm as a rock. The blow did not even stagger him, but he shook his head in silence as he **brooded**[3] on his revenge.

The other suitors were much displeased at this. One of the young men said, "Antinous, you were wrong to strike that poor wretch of a tramp. It will be worse for you if he should turn out to be some god."

---

[3] **brooded**—to be deep in thought.

Antinous paid no attention to the suitors' words. Meanwhile Telemachus was furious about the blow that had been given to his father. Though no tear fell from him, he shook his head in silence and brooded on his revenge.

In the meantime Odysseus was eating his dinner. Then Penelope called for the swineherd and said, "Eumaeus, go and tell the stranger to come here. I want to see him and ask him some questions. He seems to have traveled much. He may have seen or heard something of my husband."

To this Eumaeus answered: "You will like to hear the history of his adventures, madam. I had him with me in my hut for three days and three nights, and he has not yet completed the story of his misfortunes. I could not have been more charmed as I sat in my hut and listened to him. He says there is an old friendship between his house and that of Odysseus. He comes from Crete after having been driven here and there by every kind of misfortune. He also declares that he has heard Odysseus is alive and near at hand, and that he is bringing great wealth home with him."

"Call him here, then," said wise Penelope, "that I too may hear his story. As for the suitors, they keep hanging about our house day after day, sacrificing our oxen, sheep, and fat goats. No estate can stand such recklessness. If Odysseus were to come again, he and his son would soon have their revenge."

> *"If Odysseus were to come again, he and his son would soon have their revenge."*

As she spoke, Telemachus sneezed so loudly that the whole house echoed with it. Penelope laughed when she heard this and said to Eumaeus, "Go and call the stranger. Did you hear how my son sneezed just as I was speaking? This can only mean that all the suitors are going to be killed, and that not one of them shall escape."

Eumaeus went straight to Odysseus and said: "Stranger, my mistress Penelope has sent for you. She is in great grief, but she wishes to hear anything you can tell her about her husband."

"I will tell Penelope," answered Odysseus, "nothing but what is strictly true. I know all about her husband. I have suffered with him."

Eumaeus told Odysseus's message to Penelope. Then he went up to Telemachus and said in his ear so that none could overhear him, "My dear sir, I will now go back to the pigs, to see after your property and my own business. Be careful to keep out of danger, for there are many here who bear you ill will. May Zeus bring them to a bad end before they do us a mischief."

When Eumaeus had finished his dinner, he left and went back to his pigs. As for the suitors, they began to amuse themselves with singing and dancing, for it was now almost evening.

BOOK XVIII

*Odysseus is insulted by Irus, a beggar, who challenges
him to fight. While the suitors look on, Odysseus beats
Irus soundly.*

Now there came a certain tramp who had been begging all over the city of Ithaca. His real name was Arnaeus, but the young men called him Irus. He began to insult Odysseus.

He cried, "Be off, old man, from the doorway, or you shall be dragged out neck and heels. Do you not see that they all want me to turn you out by force? Get up then, and leave or we shall come to blows."

Odysseus frowned at him and said: "My friend, I am doing you no harm. There is room enough in this doorway for the pair of us. You seem to be just another tramp like myself, but perhaps the gods will give us better luck by and by. Do not talk too much about fighting, or you will anger me. Old though I am, I might just crack your ribs or split your lip."

Irus was very angry and answered: "You filthy pig. I have a good mind to lay both hands about you, and knock your teeth out of your head. You will never be able to fight one who is so much younger than yourself."

When Antinous saw what was going on, he laughed heartily and said to the others, "This is the finest sport that you ever saw. The stranger and Irus have quarreled and are going to fight. Let us make them do so at once."

The suitors all came up laughing and gathered round the two ragged tramps. "Listen to me," said Antinous. "There are some goats' bellies down at the fire. We have filled them with blood and fat to make a good supper pudding. He who wins shall take the one he likes. He shall feast with us from this day on, and we will not allow any other beggar about the house at all."

Odysseus tied his old rags about his hips, showing his strong thighs, his broad chest and shoulders, and his mighty arms. Athena came up to him and made his limbs even stronger still. The suitors were astonished, and said to one another, "The stranger has brought such a thigh out of his old rags that there will soon be nothing left of Irus."

Irus began to be very uneasy as he heard them. Antinous scolded him and said, "You swaggering bully. You ought never to have been born at all if you are afraid of such an old broken-down creature as this tramp is."

Then they began to fight. Irus hit Odysseus on the right shoulder, but Odysseus gave Irus a blow on the neck that broke the bones of his skull.

The servants brought him into the middle of the court, and the two men raised their hands to fight. Odysseus considered whether he should hit him so hard as to kill him, or whether he should give him a lighter blow that should only knock him down. In the end he decided to give the lighter blow for fear the Achaeans should suspect who he was. Then they began to fight. Irus hit Odysseus on the right shoulder, but Odysseus gave Irus a blow on the neck that broke the bones of his skull. The blood came gushing out of his mouth. He fell, groaning in the dust, kicking on the ground. The suitors nearly died of laughter, as Odysseus caught hold of him by the foot and dragged him into the outer court as far as the gatehouse.

Then he threw his dirty old bag over his shoulder and went back to sit down by the door. But the suitors went inside, laughing and saying to him, "May Zeus, and all the other gods grant you whatever you want for having put down this tramp."

BOOK XIX

Telemachus and Odysseus remove all armor from the court to the storeroom. Penelope talks with Odysseus, not knowing him. He tries to encourage her by telling her Odysseus will soon return. The old nurse Euryclea washes Odysseus's feet and recognizes him by a scar on his leg. She is overjoyed, but he commands her to keep silent.

A while later, Odysseus was left alone in the quiet hall, planning the ways he might kill the suitors. He said to Telemachus: "We must gather the weapons and move them to the storeroom. Make some excuse when the suitors ask you why you have removed them."

So Telemachus called nurse Euryclea and said, "Nurse, shut the women up in their rooms while I take the armor down into the storeroom."

Euryclea then locked the women inside their rooms. Odysseus and his son took the helmets, shields, and spears inside. Athena went before them with a gold lamp in her hand that shed a soft and brilliant light. And Telemachus said, "Father, the walls and roof beams are all aglow as with a white fire. Surely there is some god here who has come down from heaven."

"Hush," answered Odysseus, "hold your peace and ask no questions, for this is the manner of the gods. Go to your bed, and leave me here to talk with your mother and the maids. Your mother in her grief will ask me all sorts of questions."

On this, Telemachus went by torchlight to his room. There he lay, waiting for dawn, while in the great hall Odysseus waited by Athena's side with his mind on slaughter.

Penelope came down from her room. She asked Odysseus (still disguised as a beggar) to tell her his story.

Then she said to her head waiting-woman, "Bring a seat with a fleece, for the stranger to sit upon while he tells his story."

As soon as Odysseus had sat down, Penelope said, "Stranger, I shall first ask you who you are and where you are from. Tell me of your town and parents."

"Madam," answered Odysseus, "please ask me some other question. Do not seek to know my homeland and family. You will bring back memories that will further increase my sorrow."

Then Penelope answered: "Stranger, heaven robbed me of all beauty when the Argives set sail for Troy and my dear husband with them. If he were to return, I should be more respected and would show a better presence to the world. As it is, I am burdened with the troubles that heaven has **heaped**[1] upon me. The chiefs from all our islands are wooing me against my will and are wasting my estate. They want me to marry again at once, and I have to invent tricks in order to deceive them.

"First I set up a large weaving loom in my room. Then I said to the suitors, 'Young men, Odysseus is indeed dead. But do not press me to marry again immediately. Wait till I have finished weaving a **shroud**[2] for Laertes, to be ready at the time when death shall take him. He is very rich, and the women of the place will talk if he is laid out

> **"Stranger, heaven robbed me of all beauty when the Argives set sail for Troy and my dear husband with them."**

---

[1] **heaped**—piled.
[2] **shroud**—a cloth used to wrap a body for burial.

without one.' They agreed, so I worked at my weaving all day long. But at night I would unweave the shroud by torchlight. Every day I would bend over my loom and weave, and every night I would undo all of that day's work. I fooled them in this way for three years without their finding out. But as time wore on, those good-for-nothing maids betrayed me to the suitors. They broke in upon me and caught me unraveling a day's weaving. They were very angry with me, so I was forced to finish my work whether I wanted to or not.

"And now I do not see how I can put off marriage any longer. My son is angered at the way the suitors are eating his food. But now it is your turn to tell me who you are and from where you come."

Then Odysseus answered: "Madam, since you ask me about my family, I will answer. I come from a fair and fruitful island in mid-ocean called Crete. It is thickly peopled, and there are ninety cities on it. There is a great town there, Cnossus, where Minos reigned. Minos was father to Deucalion, whose son I am."

Odysseus told Penelope many other lies. Odysseus felt sorry for Penelope as he told her these lies, but he kept his eyes as hard as iron, holding back his tears. Then, when Penelope had stopped weeping, she turned to him again and said: "Now, stranger, I shall put you to the test. I shall see whether or not you really did know my husband and his men, as you say you did. Tell me how he was dressed. What did he look like? What were his companions like?"

"Madam," answered Odysseus, "twenty years have come and gone since he left my home. I will tell you as well as I can remember. Odysseus wore a cape of purple wool, double lined. It was fastened by a gold pin. The shirt that Odysseus wore was so soft that it fitted him like the skin of an onion."

Penelope was moved deeply as she heard Odysseus's words. She said to him: "Stranger, from now on you shall be honored and made welcome in my house. It was I who gave Odysseus the clothes you speak of. I gave him also the gold **brooch**[3] to wear as an ornament. Alas! I shall never welcome him home again. It was by an **ill fate**[4] that he ever set out for that detested city of Troy."

Then Odysseus answered: "Madam, dry your tears and listen to what I can tell you. I have lately heard that Odysseus is alive and on his way home. Zeus and the sun god were angry with him

---

[3] **brooch**—a decorative pin.

[4] **ill fate**—bad luck.

because his men had killed the sun god's cattle. His crew were all drowned. Pheidon, king of the Thesprotians, told me all this. He swore the ship was launched that would take Odysseus to his own country. So you may know he is safe and will be here shortly."

"May it be so," answered Penelope. "But I know very well that Odysseus will not return. And now, maids, wash this man's feet for him. Make him a bed on a couch with rugs and blankets, that he may be warm and quiet till morning. Then, at daybreak wash him and anoint him again, that he may sit in the hall and take his meals with Telemachus."

Penelope continued on to say, "There happens to be in the house a most respectable old woman. She is the same one who received my poor dear husband in her arms the night he was born. She nursed him in infancy. She is very feeble now, but she shall wash your feet. Come here Euryclea," said she, "and wash this poor stranger's feet."

The old woman prepared a pot of warm water for his feet. Odysseus sat by the fire, but he turned away from the light. He was worried that when the old woman saw his leg she would recognize a certain scar on it. And indeed, as soon as she began washing her master, she at once knew the scar. It was one that had been given him by a wild boar when he was hunting.

Joy filled her heart. Euryclea's eyes filled with tears, and she said, "My dear child, I am sure you must be Odysseus himself. I did not know you until I had actually touched the scar."

Odysseus drew Euryclea close to him and said, "Nurse, though you have recognized me, hold your tongue, and do not say a word about it to anyone else in the house. For if you do, I will not spare your life, though you are my own nurse."

"My child," answered Euryclea, "you know very well that nothing can either bend or break me. I will hold my tongue like a stone or a piece of iron."

When she had washed him and anointed him with oil, Odysseus drew his seat nearer to the fire to warm himself and hid the scar under his rags. Then Penelope began talking to him and said:

"Listen to a dream that I have had and interpret it for me if you can." Penelope dreamed about twenty geese killed by a great eagle.

"This dream," replied Odysseus, "can only have one meaning. The death of the suitors is foretold. Not one of them will escape."

And Penelope answered: "Stranger, dreams are very curious things, and they do not always come true. Tomorrow will be the sad day that I leave the house of Odysseus. Tomorrow I plan to hold a tournament of axes. My husband used to set up twelve axes in the court, one in front of the other. He would then go back from them and shoot an arrow through the whole twelve. I shall make the suitors try to do the same thing. Whoever can string the bow most easily and send his arrow through all twelve axes will be the one whom I follow. I will leave this house of my husband."

> *"Now I must go upstairs and lie upon that bed that I have flooded with my tears from the day Odysseus left."*

Then Odysseus answered, "Madam, Odysseus will return before they can string the bow and send their arrows through the iron."

To this Penelope said, "Now I must go upstairs and lie upon that bed that I have flooded with my tears from the day Odysseus left."

BOOK XX

At the feast, Telemachus seats the ragged Odysseus in an honorable place. But Odysseus is again abused by the suitors. The stranger Theoclymenus, seeing signs of disaster near, takes his leave.

O dysseus lay awake brooding all night on the way in which he should kill the suitors. By and by, Athena came down from heaven in the form of a woman. She hovered over his head, saying, "My poor unhappy man, why do you lie awake in this way?"

"Goddess," answered Odysseus, "I am worried about how I shall be able to kill these wicked suitors single-handed. There are so many of them. And even if I succeed in killing them, where am I to escape from their **avengers**[1] when it is all over?"

---

[1] **avengers**—persons who seek revenge on behalf of people killed or hurt.

"For shame," replied Athena, "am I not a goddess? Have I not protected you throughout in all your troubles? Go to sleep and do not worry. Your troubles shall be over before long."

As she spoke, she rained soft sleep over his eyes and then went back to Olympus.

At daybreak Odysseus heard the sound of Penelope weeping. He then went out to the place where the Achaeans were meeting in assembly. Shortly after, the swineherd arrived with the three fat pigs.

Melanthius the goatherd brought in his best goats for the suitors' dinner. Melanthius began insulting Odysseus. "Are you still here, stranger," said he, "to bother people by begging about the house? Why can you not go elsewhere? Do you need a beating to help you understand?"

Odysseus made no answer but bowed his head and brooded.

Meanwhile the suitors were plotting to murder Telemachus. But a bird flew near them on their left hand, an eagle with a dove in its claws. On seeing this, Amphinomus said, "My friends, this plot to murder Telemachus will not succeed. Let us go to dinner instead."

The others agreed, so they went inside and sat down to dinner.

Telemachus gave Odysseus a seat at a little table by himself just by the door of the hall. "Sit there," said he, "and drink your wine among the great people. I will put a stop to the insults and blows of the suitors, for this house belongs to Odysseus and has passed from him to me. Suitors, keep your hands and your tongues to yourselves, or there will be trouble."

The suitors marveled at the boldness of his speech. They roasted the meat, gave every man a part, and feasted to their hearts' content. Those who served the meat gave Odysseus exactly the same amount as the others had, for Telemachus had told them to do so.

Telemachus paid no attention to the suitors who were insulting his father. He sat silently watching his father, expecting every moment that he would begin his attack upon the suitors.

Meanwhile, Penelope had a seat placed for her facing the court and halls so that she could hear what everyone was saying. She heard the crowd laugh as they continued their dinner, which was a feast, for many animals were killed. But Athena and Odysseus would soon lay before the suitors a gruesome meal, for they had filled that house with pain.

BOOK XXI

*After the banquet is over, Penelope brings out Odysseus's
bow. First Telemachus and then the suitors try to string
it without success. Odysseus reveals himself to Eumaeus
and Philoetius, the stockman. They bar the outer doors
and send the women to their rooms in preparation for
the fighting. Odysseus strings the bow with ease and
shoots it with perfection. The suitors watch him, with fear
and dismay.*

Athena now put it in Penelope's mind to make
the suitors try their skill with the bow and with the
iron axes. Penelope went with her maidens into
the storeroom and took down the bow from the
peg on which it hung. She took the bow out of its
case. When her tears had stopped, she went to the
hall where the suitors were, carrying the bow and

the **quiver**,[1] with the many deadly arrows that were inside it. When she reached the suitors, Penelope said:

"Listen to me, suitors, my lords. I will bring out the mighty bow of Odysseus. Whoever can string it most easily and send his arrow through each one of twelve axes will be the one I follow and for whom I will leave this house of my lawful husband."

She told Eumaeus to set the bow and the pieces of iron before the suitors.

Then Telemachus spoke. "Come, then, make no excuses for delay. Let us see whether or not you can string the bow. I too will try it. If I can string it and shoot through the iron, my heart will be less heavy when my mother leaves."

As he spoke, he jumped up from his seat. First he set the axes in a row, in a long groove that he had dug for them. Then he stamped the earth tight round them and attempted to string the bow.

─────────

"Listen to me, suitors, my lords. I will bring out the mighty bow of Odysseus. Whoever can string it most easily and send his arrow through each one of twelve axes will be the one I follow and for whom I will leave this house of my lawful husband."

─────────

---

[1] **quiver**—portable case for holding arrows.

Three times did he tugged at it, trying with all his might to draw the string. Three times he failed. He was trying for the fourth time when a signal from Odysseus made him stop. So he said:

"Alas! I shall either be always weak, or I am too young and have not yet reached my full strength. You others go ahead and try the bow and get this contest settled."

Leiodes, son of Oenops, was the first to rise. But he could not string the bow, for his hands were weak and not used to hard work.

He put the bow down and took his seat again. Antinous scolded him, saying:

"Leiodes, what are you thinking about? You were not born to be an archer, but there are others who will soon string it."

Then he said to Melanthius the goatherd, "Bring us also a large ball of fat. Let us warm the bow and grease it. We will then try it again and bring the contest to an end."

The suitors warmed the bow and again tried it, but none of them was nearly strong enough to string it.

Eumaeus the swineherd and Philoetius the stockman left the hall now together, and Odysseus followed them. When they had got outside the gates, Odysseus said to them quietly:

"Stockman, and you, swineherd, I have a question to ask you. If some god should bring Odysseus back here all of a sudden, would you side with the suitors, or with Odysseus?"

"Father Zeus," answered the stockman, "if some god were to bring Odysseus back, I would fight for him with all my strength."

In like words Eumaeus prayed to all the gods that Odysseus might return. When Odysseus saw how loyal they felt toward him, he said: "It is I, Odysseus, who am here. I have suffered much, but at last, in the twentieth year, I have come back to my own country. I find that you two alone of all my servants are glad that I should do so. I have not heard any of the others praying for my return. To you two, therefore, will I tell the truth."

Both men were overjoyed to see him again and began weeping. Then Odysseus said:

"Stop your weeping. The suitors will all try to prevent me from getting hold of the bow and quiver. Eumaeus, you place it in my hands when you are carrying it about. Tell the women to close their doors. If they hear any sound of men fighting about the house, they must not come out. And I command you, Philoetius, to lock the doors of the outer gate."

Then Odysseus went back into the house and took the seat. Soon after, his two servants followed him inside.

At this moment, Eurymachus was warming the bow by the fire, but he still could not string it. He sighed and said, "I shall not be able to marry Penelope. But I am ashamed most of our being so inferior to Odysseus in strength that we cannot string his bow. This will disgrace us in the eyes of those who are yet unborn."

"It shall not be so, Eurymachus," said Antinous. "Today is the feast of Apollo. Who can string a bow on such a day as this? Let us make our drink offerings and drop this matter of the bow."

The rest approved his words, so they all made their drink offerings. Then Odysseus said:

"Suitors of the queen, give me the bow so I may see whether I still have as much strength as I used to have."

This made them all very angry, for they feared he might string the bow. They scolded him fiercely, saying: "You will find no mercy from anyone here if you string the bow."

Penelope then spoke to Antinous. "If this stranger proves strong enough to string the mighty bow of Odysseus, where do you suppose he would take me home with him and make me his wife?"

"Queen Penelope," answered Eurymachus, "we do not suppose that this man will take you away with him. But we are afraid that some of the Achaeans should go about gossiping and say, 'These suitors are a feeble folk. They are paying court to the wife of a brave man whose bow not one of them was able to string. Yet a beggarly tramp who came to the house strung it at once and sent an arrow through the iron.' This is what will be said, and it will be a scandal against us."

"Eurymachus," Penelope answered, "why should you mind if men talk as you think they will? This stranger is strong and well built. Give him the bow, and let us see whether he can string it or not. If Apollo grants him the glory of stringing it, I will give him a cloak and shirt, a spear to keep off dogs and robbers, and a sharp sword. I will also give him sandals and will see him sent safely wherever he wants to go."

Then Telemachus said: "Mother, I am the only one who has the right to let anyone have the bow or to refuse it. Go within the house and busy yourself with your daily duties. This bow is a man's matter, and mine above all others, for it is I who am master here."

She went wondering back into the house. Going upstairs with her handmaids into her room, she mourned her dear husband till Athena sent sweet sleep over her eyelids.

The swineherd Eumaeus brought the bow and placed it in the hands of Odysseus. Odysseus carefully examined the bow to see whether the worms had been eating into it while he was away.

When he had examined it all over, he strung it as easily as a skilled **bard**[2] strings a new peg of his **lyre**.[3] Then he took it in his right hand to test the string. It sang sweetly under his touch. The suitors were dismayed and turned pale as they heard it. At that moment, Zeus thundered loudly, and the heart of Odysseus rejoiced as he heard the **omen**.[4]

He took an arrow that was lying upon the table and laid it on the bow. He drew the arrow and the string toward him, still seated on his seat. When he had taken aim, he let the arrow fly. His arrow pierced every one of the handle-holes of the axes from the first onward till it had gone right through them and into the outer courtyard. Then he said to Telemachus:

---

[2] **bard**—poet, often one who sings.

[3] **lyre**—a stringed instrument of the harp family.

[4] **omen**—sign from the gods of future events.

"Your guest has not disgraced you, Telemachus. I did not miss what I aimed at, and I was not long in stringing my bow."

As he spoke, he made a sign with his eyebrows to Telemachus, who then fastened his sword, grasped his spear, and stood armed beside his father's seat.

BOOK XXII

Odysseus tears off his rags and begins the slaughter of the suitors. Telemachus brings armor from the storeroom. Athena appears to help Odysseus. The suitors try to defend themselves, but all finally are killed. Odysseus learns from Euryclea which of the housemaids have been guilty of misbehavior, and these are hanged.

Then Odysseus tore off his rags and sprang up with his bow and his quiver full of arrows. He said, "The mighty contest is at an end. I will now see whether Apollo will allow me to hit another mark that no man has yet hit."

On this he aimed a deadly arrow at Antinous, who was about to drink his wine. The arrow struck Antinous in the throat, and the point went clean through his neck. He fell over and the cup dropped from his hand. A thick stream of blood gushed from his nose. He kicked the table from him and upset the bread and meat on it, which fell over on the ground.

The suitors were in an uproar when they saw that a man had been hit. They sprang in dismay from their seats and scolded Odysseus angrily. "Stranger," said they, "you shall pay for shooting people in this way. Antinous was the most important youth in Ithaca."

But Odysseus glared at them and said: "Dogs, did you think that I should not come back from Troy? You have forced yourself upon this house, and have wooed my wife while I was still living. You have feared neither god nor man, and now you shall die."

They turned pale with fear as he spoke. Every man looked round about to see whether he might fly for safety. Eurymachus alone spoke.

"If you are Odysseus," said he, "then what you have said is fair. We have done much wrong on

"Dogs, did you think that I should not come back from Troy? You have forced yourself upon this house, and have wooed my wife while I was still living. You have feared neither god nor man, and now you shall die."

your lands and in your house. But Antinous was our leader. It was all his doing. It was not that he wanted to marry Penelope. He wanted to kill your son and to be chief man in Ithaca. Now that he has met death, spare the lives of your people. We will pay you for all that we have eaten. We will keep on giving you gold and bronze till your heart is softened."

Odysseus again glared at him and said: "Even if you should give me all you have in the world, I will not stop till I have paid all of you in full."

Their hearts sank as they heard him, but Eurymachus again spoke saying:

"My friends, this man will kill every man among us. Let us then fight. Draw your swords, and hold up the tables to shield you from his arrows."

As he spoke, he drew his blade of bronze and with a loud cry sprang toward Odysseus. But Odysseus instantly shot an arrow into his breast that fixed itself in his liver. Eurymachus dropped his sword and fell, doubled up, over his table. The cup and all the meats fell to the ground. He hit the earth with his forehead in the agonies of death.

Amphinomus next drew his sword and tried to get Odysseus away from the door. But Telemachus was too quick for him and struck him from behind. The spear caught him between the shoulders and went right through his chest. He fell heavily to the ground and struck the earth with his forehead. Then Telemachus sprang away from him and ran to his father's side, saying:

"Father, let me bring you a shield, two spears, and a brass helmet. I will arm myself as well and will bring other armor for the swineherd and the stockman."

"Run and fetch them," answered Odysseus, "while my arrows hold out." Telemachus ran off to the storeroom where the armor was kept. He chose four shields, eight spears, and four brass helmets. Meanwhile

Meanwhile Odysseus had been shooting the suitors one by one, and they fell on top of one another.

Odysseus had been shooting the suitors one by one, and they fell on top of one another. When his arrows gave out, he set the bow to stand by the doorpost. He hung a shield that was four hides thick about his shoulders. On his head he set his helmet, well made with a crest of horsehair that nodded **menacingly**[1] above it. He grasped two bronze spears.

At one end of the pavement, there was an exit leading to a narrow hall. This exit was blocked by a well-made door. Odysseus told Philoetius the stockman to stand by this door and guard it, for only one person could attack it at a time. But Agelaus shouted, "Cannot someone go up to the window and tell the people outside what is going on? Help would come at once. We should soon make an end of this man and his arrows."

"This may not be, Agelaus," answered Melanthius. "The mouth of the narrow passage is dangerously near the entrance to the outer court. One brave man could prevent any number from getting in. But I know what I will do: I will bring you arms from the storeroom, for I am sure it is there that Odysseus and his son have put them."

Then Melanthius went by a back hall to the storeroom. There he chose twelve shields, with as many helmets and spears, and brought them back as fast as he could to give them to the suitors. Odysseus's heart began to fail him when he saw the suitors putting on their armor and waving their

---

[1] **menacingly**—threateningly.

spears. He said to Telemachus, "Some one of the women inside is helping the suitors against us, or it may be Melanthius."

Telemachus answered: "The fault, father, is mine. I left the storeroom door open, and they have kept a sharper lookout than I have. Go, Eumaeus, and see whether it is one of the women who is doing this, or whether, as I suspect, it is Melanthius."

Meanwhile Melanthius was again going to the storeroom to fetch more armor. But the swineherd saw him and said to Odysseus, "Odysseus, it is that scoundrel Melanthius, just as we suspected, who is going to the storeroom. Shall I kill him myself, or shall I bring him here that you may take your own revenge for all the many wrongs that he has done in your house?"

Odysseus answered: "Telemachus and I will hold these suitors in check, no matter what they do. Go back, both of you, and tie Melanthius's hands and feet behind him. Throw him into the storeroom and close the door behind you. Lash him to a plank, and tie him to the roof beams. Let him live on there, suffering."

So Eumaeus and Philoetius went to the storeroom and took their stand outside the door. By and by, Melanthius came out with a helmet in one hand

and an old dry-rotted shield in the other. The two men grabbed him, dragged him back by the hair, and threw him struggling to the ground. They bent his hands and feet behind his back and bound them tight. Then they fastened him and tied him up from a high pillar. Eumaeus said, "Melanthius, you will pass the night on as soft a bed as you deserve."

There, then, they left him to die and went back to take their places by the side of Odysseus. The four men stood by the door, fierce and full of fury.

Meanwhile Agelaus, Eurynomus, Amphimedon, Demoptolemus, Pisander, and Polybus, son of Polyctor, were the leaders of the fight on the suitors' side. They were by far the most courageous. The others had already fallen under the arrows of Odysseus. Agelaus shouted to them and said: "My friends, six of you throw your spears first. See if you cannot cover yourselves with glory by killing him. When he has fallen, we need not worry about the others."

They threw their spears, but Athena let none of them hit Odysseus and his men. Odysseus said to his own men, "My friends, we too had better throw our spears, or they will kill us outright."

They aimed straight in front of them and threw their spears. Odysseus killed Demoptolemus, Telemachus killed Euryades, and Eumaeus killed Elatus, while the stockman killed Pisander. As the others drew back into a corner, Odysseus and his men rushed forward and took their spears by drawing them out of the bodies of the dead.

The suitors now aimed a second time. Again Athena made their weapons miss their mark. Still, Amphimedon took a piece of the top skin from off Telemachus's wrist, and Ctesippus managed to graze Eumaeus's shoulder above his shield. Then Odysseus, his son, the swineherd, and the stockman aimed their weapons into the crowd of suitors. Odysseus hit Eurydamas, Telemachus hit Amphimedon, and Eumaeus hit Polybus. The stockman hit Ctesippus in the chest.

Odysseus struck the son of Damastor with a spear in a close fight. Telemachus hit Leocritus in the belly. The dart went clean through him, so that he fell forward on his face upon the ground. Then Athena from her seat on the rafter held up her deadly shield. The suitors shrank back in fear. They fled to the other end of the court like a herd of cattle. Odysseus and his men fell upon the suitors and hit them on every side. They made a horrible groaning as their brains were being battered in. The ground was soaked with their blood.

Leiodes then caught the knees of Odysseus and said, "Odysseus, I beg you have mercy upon me and spare me. I never wronged any of the women in your house either in word or deed. I tried to stop the others, but they would not listen. Now they are paying for their sins. I was their priest. If you kill me, I shall die without having done anything to deserve it. I shall have gotten no thanks for all the good that I did."

Odysseus looked at him and answered, "You must have prayed many a time that I would never get home again, and that you might marry my wife. Therefore you shall die."

With these words he picked up the sword that Agelaus had dropped when he was being killed. Then he struck Leiodes on the back of his neck, so his head fell rolling in the dust while he was yet speaking.

The musician Phemius, who had been forced by the suitors to sing to them, now tried to save his life. He laid his lyre on the ground, then going up to Odysseus, he caught hold of his knees and said: "Odysseus, I beg you have mercy on me and spare me. Your own son Telemachus will tell you that I did not want to sing to the suitors after their meals. But they were too many and too strong for me, so they made me."

Telemachus heard him and went up to his father. "Stop!" he cried. "The man is guiltless. Do him no harm. We will spare the **herald**,[2] Medon too, who was always good to me when I was a boy."

Medon heard these words of Telemachus, for he was under a chair. He went up to Telemachus and laid hold of his knees.

"Fear not! Telemachus has saved your life. Go and be out of the way of the slaughter while I finish my work here inside."

"Here I am, my dear sir," said he. "Tell your father, or he will kill me in his rage against the suitors."

Odysseus smiled at him and answered, "Fear not! Telemachus has saved your life. Go and be out of the way of the slaughter while I finish my work here inside."

---

[2] **herald**—messenger.

The pair went into the outer court as fast as they could, looking fearfully round, and still expecting that they would be killed. Then Odysseus searched the whole court, to see if anyone had managed to hide. He found all the suitors dead, lying in the dust and soaking in their blood.

Then Odysseus said to Telemachus, "Call nurse Euryclea. I have something to say to her."

Telemachus went and knocked at the door of the women's room. "Come outside," said he, "my father wishes to speak to you."

When she saw all the blood, she began to cry out for joy, for she saw that a great deed had been done.

Euryclea unfastened the door of the women's room and came out, following Telemachus. She found Odysseus among the bodies spattered with blood. When she saw all the blood, she began to cry out for joy, for she saw that a great deed had been done. But Odysseus hushed her. "Old woman," said he, "rejoice in silence. It is an unholy thing to brag over dead men. Heaven's doom and their own evil deeds have brought these men to destruction. They have come to a bad end as a punishment for their wickedness and folly. Now tell me which of the women in the house have dishonored me by their behavior and their speech, and who are innocent."

"I will tell you the truth, my son," answered Euryclea. "There are fifty women trained by your lady and myself in household work. Of these, twelve have been disloyal."

Odysseus said, "Tell the women who have been disloyal to come to me."

Euryclea left the room to tell the women. In the meantime, Odysseus called Telemachus, the stockman, and the swineherd. "Begin," said he, "to remove the dead, and make the twelve women help you. Then, get sponges and clean water to wipe down the tables and seats. When you have thoroughly cleansed the whole hall, take the women outside and hang them."

The twelve women who had dishonored Odysseus's house came down together, weeping and wailing bitterly. First they carried the dead bodies out and propped them up against one another in the gatehouse. Odysseus ordered them about to carry out the bodies. When they had done this, they cleaned all the tables and seats with sponges and water. Telemachus and the two others shoveled up the blood and dirt from the ground. The women carried it all away and put it outdoors. Then, when the whole place was quite clean and orderly, Telemachus took the women out to the narrow space between the wall of the room and that of the yard, so that they could not get away. He then said to the other two, "I shall not let these women die a clean death. They were insolent to me and my mother, and they slept with the suitors."

He tied a ship's cable tightly to one of the posts that supported the roof. He tied it at a good height, so that the women's feet would not touch the ground. Then he put their heads in nooses one after the other and hanged them. The handmaids died most miserably. Their feet kicked for a while, but not for very long.

As for Melanthius, they took him outside, and there they cut off his nose and his ears. Then, in their fury, they cut off his hands and his feet.

When they had done this, they washed their hands and feet and went back into the house. Odysseus said to the dear old nurse Euryclea, "Bring me sulfur, which cleanses all. Then go and tell Penelope to come here with her attendants and all the maidservants who are in the house."

Euryclea brought the fire and sulfur, as he had asked her. Odysseus thoroughly cleaned the hall. Then Euryclea went inside to call the women and tell them what had happened. They came from their rooms with torches in their hands and pressed round Odysseus to embrace him. They kissed his head and shoulders and took hold of his hands. It made him feel like weeping, for he remembered every one of them, even after twenty years.

BOOK XXIII

Euryclea now tells her mistress that the beggar who has killed the suitors is Odysseus. Unbelieving, Penelope questions him, and is at last convinced. They embrace and talk happily through much of the night. The following day Odysseus goes to tell his father Laertes of his return.

Euryclea now went upstairs laughing, to tell Penelope that her dear husband had come home. Her aged knees became young again and her feet were nimble for joy as she bent over Penelope's head to speak to her. "Wake up, Penelope, my dear child," she exclaimed. "See with your own eyes something that you have been wanting for a long time. Odysseus has at last come home again. He has killed the suitors who were giving so much trouble in his house."

"My good nurse," answered Penelope, "you must be mad. Why should you mock me when I have trouble enough already?"

"My dear child," answered Euryclea, "I am not mocking you. It is true that Odysseus has come home again. He was the stranger they were all treating so badly. Telemachus knew all the time, but he kept his father's secret so Odysseus might have his revenge on all these wicked people."

Then Penelope got up from her couch, threw her arms round Euryclea, and wept for joy. On this Penelope came down from her room. When she had crossed the stone floor of the hall, she sat down with Odysseus by the fire. Odysseus sat looking upon the ground, waiting to see what his brave wife would say to him when she saw him. For a long time she sat silent, lost in amazement. Even though she looked him full in the face, she was misled by his shabby clothes and wasn't sure she recognized him. Telemachus began to scold her and said:

"Mother, why do you keep away from father in this way? No other woman could keep away from her husband when he h back to her after twenty years."

Penelope answered: "My son, I can find no words. I cannot even look him straight in the face. Still, if he really is Odysseus, I shall soon find out. For there are things that we two alone know about and that are hidden from all others."

Odysseus smiled at this and said to Telemachus: "Let your mother put me to any proof she likes. She believes me to be somebody else, because I am covered with dirt and have on such ragged clothes."

"Let me think what will be best," continued Odysseus. "First wash and put on clean clothes. Word about the deaths of the suitors will get about in the town, before we can escape to the woods upon my own land. Once there, we will decide which course of action seems wisest."

The maidservant Eurynome washed and anointed Odysseus and gave him a shirt and cloak. Athena made him look taller and stronger than before. He came from the bath looking like one of the gods and sat down opposite his wife. "My dear," said he, "no other woman could bear to keep away from her husband when he had come back to her after twenty years. Come, nurse, get a bed ready. I will sleep alone, for this woman has a heart of iron."

"**M**y dear," answered Penelope, "I very well remember what kind of a man you were when you set sail from Ithaca. Euryclea, take his bed outside the bedchamber that he himself built. Bring the bed outside this room, and put bedding upon it with fleeces, good **coverlets,**[1] and blankets."

She said this to test him, but Odysseus was very angry and said: "Wife, I am much displeased with you. Who dared to move my bed? He must have found it a hard task, no matter how skilled a workman he was. There is no man living, however strong, who could move it from its place.

"There was a young olive growing within the house. I built my room round this tree with strong walls of stone and a roof. Then I cut off the top branches of the olive tree and left the stump standing. I then drilled a hole down the middle and made it the centerpost of my bed. After this, I stretched a hide of leather from one side of it to the other. So, you see, I know all about it. I wish to know whether it is still there, or whether anyone has been removing it by cutting down the olive tree at its roots."

When Penelope heard this, she fairly down. She flew weeping to his side, flung about his neck, and kissed him. "Do r

---

[1] **coverlets**—bedspreads.

with me, Odysseus," she cried, "you, who are the wisest of men. We have suffered, both of us. Heaven has denied us the happiness of growing old together. Do not then be angry that I did not embrace you as soon as I saw you. I have been shuddering all the time through fear that someone might come here and deceive me."

At last, Odysseus said: "Wife, we have not yet reached the end of our troubles. I have a lot of work still to do. But now let us go to bed, that we may lie down and enjoy blessed sleep."

Penelope replied, "First tell what lies before you."

"My dear," answered Odysseus, "I will not hide it from you, though you will not like it. The prophet Teiresias told me to travel far and wide, carrying an oar, till I came to a country where the people have never heard of the sea and do not even \`ix salt with their food. They know nothing about 's nor oars. He said that a traveler would meet \`d ask me whether it was a winnowing fan \`d on my shoulder. On this, I was to stick the ground and sacrifice a ram, a bull, anc Poseidon. After this, I was to go home myse. 'ces to all the gods in heaven. As for at death would come to me from the sea. My life would **ebb**[2] away very gently when I was full of years and had peace of mind, and my people would bless me."

And Penelope said, "If the gods are going to grant you a happier time in your old age, you may hope then to have some relief from your sorrows."

After Odysseus and Penelope had had their fill of love, they began talking with one another. She told him how much she had had to bear in seeing the house filled with a crowd of wicked suitors. Odysseus told her what he had suffered, and how much trouble he had given to other people. He told her everything, and she was so delighted to listen that she never went to sleep till he had ended his whole story. Finally, a deep sleep took hold of Odysseus.

After Odysseus had had enough rest, he said, "I am now going to the wooded lands out in th country to see my father, who has so long b sad on my account. At sunrise, word will s that I have been killing the suitors. Go therefore, and stay there with your wom

> *"If the gods are going to grant you a happier time in your old age, you may hope then to have some relief from your sorrows."*

---

[2] **ebb**—fall away, decline.

BOOK XXIV

The ghosts of the suitors gather miserably in the house of Hades. Meanwhile, Odysseus finds his father working humbly in his orchard and reveals himself to Laertes. Certain men of Ithaca, seeking to avenge the suitors, march to attack Odysseus. The battle begins, but Athena stops it, bidding them to make peace.

Hades, the place of the dead, the ghosts of

itors were gathered.

od Hermes came to them. The ghosts of

n and Achilles were astonished at seeing

and it to them at once.

brought suitors said, "I will tell you fully

bout the way our end was

He then told the whole story of how the suitors courted Odysseus's wife and wasted his estate until Odysseus finally returned and killed them all.

"This, Agamemnon, is how we came by our end," concluded the ghost of one suitor. "Our bodies are lying still uncared for in the house of Odysseus. Our friends at home do not yet know what has happened."

Thus did they tell what happened in the house of Hades, deep down within the earth where Death is lord. Meanwhile, Odysseus and the others went out of the town to the farm of Laertes. When Odysseus got there, he said to his son and to the other two:

"Go to the house, and kill the best pig that you can find for dinner. Meanwhile I want to see whether my father will recognize me after so long."

Odysseus turned off into the vineyard to put his father to a test. He found his father alone. He had on a dirty old shirt, patched and very shabby. When Odysseus saw him so worn, so old and full of sorrow, he stood still under a tall pear tree and began to weep. He wanted to hold him and tell him all about his having come home. Yet he decided to first question him and see what he would say. He went up to his father and said: "I see, sir, that you are an excellent gardener. You seem to take better care of your garden than of yourself. But tell me, in whose garden are you working? Tell me, is this place that I have come to really Ithaca?

His father answered: "Sir, you have indeed come to Ithaca, but it is fallen into the hands of wicked people. But now, tell me truly: Who are you? Tell me of your town and parents. What ship has brought you and your men to Ithaca?"

"I will tell you everything," answered Odysseus. The heart of Odysseus was deeply touched as he looked upon his father. He decided to tell him the truth. Then he sprang toward him, flung his arms about him, and kissed him, saying, "I am he, father, about whom you are asking! I have returned after being away for twenty years. But stop your grieving. We have no time to lose. I have killed the suitors in my house to punish them for their crimes."

"If you really are my son Odysseus," replied Laertes, "you must give me some proof."

"First observe this scar," answered Odysseus, "which I got from a boar's tusk when I was hunting on Mount Parnassus."

Laertes's strength failed him when he heard the proofs that his son had given him. He threw his arms about Odysseus.

The two then made their way toward the house. When they got there, they found Telemachus with the stockman and the swineherd cutting up meat and mixing wine with water. Then an old woman took Laertes inside and washed him and anointed him with oil. She put a good cloak on him.

When the feast was ready, each man took his proper place on the benches and seats and began eating.

Meanwhile, the news went round the town about the terrible fate that had happened to the suitors. As soon as the people heard of it, they gathered from everywhere, groaning before the house of Odysseus. They took the dead away and buried them. They then met angrily in the center of town. Eupeithes rose to speak. He was overwhelmed with grief at the death of his son Antinous. So he said, weeping bitterly: "My friend, this man has done the Achaeans great wrong. He took many of our best men away with him in his fleet, and he has lost both ships and men. Now, on his return, he has been killing all our sons and brothers. It will be a disgrace to us if we do not avenge these murders. Let us be after them before they can leave the land."

**"Men of Ithaca,
it is your own fault
that things
have turned out
as they have.
You would not listen
to me when we
told you to stop
the wrong your sons
were doing. Do
not go out against
Odysseus, or you
may bring evil
upon yourselves."**

On hearing this, old Halitherses rose to speak, for he was the only man among them who knew both past and future. So he spoke to them in all honesty, saying:

"Men of Ithaca, it is your own fault that things have turned out as they have. You would not listen to me when we told you to stop the wrong your sons were doing. Do not go out against Odysseus, or you may bring evil upon yourselves."

More than half the men raised a loud shout of approval, but the rest stayed where they were. They hurried off for their armor. Then they met together in front of the city.

Meanwhile, the gods of Mt. Olympus looked on. Athena said to Zeus, "Father, what do you propose to do? Will you set them fighting still further, or will you make peace between them?"

And Zeus answered: "My child, why should you ask me? Was it not by your own arrangement that Odysseus came home and took his revenge upon the suitors? Do whatever you like, but I will tell you what I think is best. Now that Odysseus is revenged, let them swear he will continue to rule. Let us cause the others to forget the massacre of their sons and brothers. Let them all become friends as before, and let peace and plenty reign."

This was what Athena was already eager to bring about. So down she darted from the topmost **summit**[1] of Olympus to join Odysseus.

When Laertes and the others had finished dinner, Odysseus said, "Some of you go out and see if the people out to avenge the deaths of the suitors are getting close to us." Laertes replied, "Here they are. Let us put on our armor at once."

They put on their armor as fast as they could. Then they opened the gate and went forth, Odysseus leading the way.

Then Athena came up to them. Odysseus was glad when he saw her. He said to his son, "Telemachus, you are about to fight in a battle that will show every man's character. Be sure not to disgrace your ancestors, who were famous for their strength and courage."

---

[1] **summit**—the highest point, the top.

Odysseus and his son fell upon the front line of the enemy and hit them with their swords and spears. Indeed, they would have killed every one of them, but Athena raised her voice and made everyone pause. "Men of Ithaca," she cried, "stop this dreadful war, and settle the matter at once without further bloodshed. Make peace!"

Her words frightened everyone. Their weapons dropped from their hands and fell upon the ground at the sound of the goddess's voice. They fled back to the city for their lives. But Odysseus gave a great cry and was about to follow the suitors' avengers. Then Zeus sent a thunderbolt of fire that fell just in front of Athena, as a sign. She said to Odysseus, "Odysseus, noble son of Laertes, stop this warful strife, or Zeus will be angry with you."

Thus spoke Athena, and Odysseus obeyed her. She made a peace agreement between the two warring parties.